"It's your fault the Holy Land was destroyed..."
"We lost everything!"
"DIIIIIIE!!!"

CONTENTS

I SHALL SURVIVE USING POTIONS!

Design
Hyakuashiya Yuuko + Tanigome Kabuto
(musicagographics)

I SHALL SURVIVE USING P TIONS! 2

Author **FUNA** Illust. **Sukima**

Holy Land
of Rueda

Mountain
Range

Grua

Aligot
Empire

Balmore

Aras

Drisard

Aseed

Brancott

Litenia

Jursal

I SHALL SURVIVE USING POTIONS!

2

Author: FUNA
Illustrator: Sukima

I Shall Survive Using Potions! Volume 2
by FUNA

Translated by Garrison Denim
Edited by CHaSE and William Haggard
Layout by Leah Waig
English Cover & Lettering by Kelsey Denton

Copyright © 2017 FUNA
Illustrations by Sukima

First published in Japan in 2017 by Kodansha Ltd., Tokyo.
Publication rights for this English edition arranged through Kodansha Ltd., Tokyo.

Find more books like this one at www.j-novel.club!

President and Publisher: Samuel Pinansky
Managing Editor (Novels): Aimee Zink
QA Manager: Hannah N. Carter
Marketing Manager: Stephanie Hii
Project Managers: Chi Tran & Michael Meeker

ISBN: 978-1-7183-7191-0
Printed in Korea
First Printing: October 2020
10 9 8 7 6 5 4 3 2 1

Chapter 8:
Visitors

Fernand, crown prince of the Kingdom of Brancott, had a glum look on his face. After Fabio and Allan visited the restaurant Kaoru had worked at the day after the prince's disastrous party, they came saying they hadn't seen her. The staff there said that she might not be coming back at all since she received a summons from some bigwig, so the two had given up and went home so as to not cause any trouble.

She actually skipped town? Is that really how far into a corner I drove her...?

After looking into where she could have gone, they found several eyewitness accounts of a girl covered in blood heading toward the city gates. The guard by the gate confirmed the story, adding in his own testimony that the girl didn't have much in the way of baggage when she left.

Did she make it to another town all right? Would she be able to find more work with a wound like that?

The more he thought about it, the heavier his heart became...

"I heard something interesting, Fernand," Fabio said as he entered the room, a tinge of excitement in his voice. Considering how calm and collected he usually was, it was rare to see him like this.

"What are you talking about?" Fernand asked, his curiosity slightly piqued.

"Try not to be too surprised, alright? This is something I heard from a merchant who just got back to the capital from Grua. Apparently, there's a girl there who claims to be a friend of the Goddess Celestine; she can create miracles and has been helping people. She also did quite a number on the temple and the king."

"What the heck is that all about?" Fernand balked. He couldn't believe that Fabio was actually taken in by that story. It was outrageous enough that even calling it gossip seemed far-fetched.

"So, about that supposed friend of the Goddess…"

He doesn't know when to quit…

"She looks about eleven or twelve years old, with black hair and black eyes."

…Wait, what was that?

"And it appears her name is Kaoru."

"Think up a reason for us to go to Balmore! Government affairs, a courtesy visit, I don't care what! Just make it so we can get going now!"

"I thought you might say that, so I already took the liberty of making preparations beforehand…"

Way to go, Fabio!

"Alright then, let's get out there and bring her back! Things are probably pretty dicey for her if she's managed to pick a fight with both the temple *and* the king. This is the perfect chance to make our move!"

Though he had more or less reflected on what he had done wrong before, it seemed like Fernand's habit of jumping into action when things looked good *only* for him wasn't going to be fixed anytime soon.

"Man, it sure is peaceful around here…"

Life for me became pretty quiet and uneventful after the dust had settled. I was a little worried that some of the more thick-headed people were going to come after me after such a public event. Like nobles, or… Well, just nobles, really. It looked like my threats worked, though, as I wasn't really getting any unwanted visitors.

Even if someone had captured me or tried forcing me to do anything, there wasn't any point. Miracles had to pass through the Goddess, after all, which meant she would figure out what was going on in a heartbeat. There was no one out there who thought the Goddess would let anyone get away with taking me hostage.

I *did* say that Celes might come down and decimate the capital and everyone in it if they tried pulling anything, so I'm sure the higher-ups must have been pretty clear on drilling the idea into everyone's heads that no one better lay a finger on me. I figured that, after the royal family and the nobility weighed the pros and cons, and considered the risk versus reward of forcibly getting into contact with me, they must have realized it just wasn't worth it.

The same went for the temple as well. There wasn't a single person who didn't know who they were, which meant they couldn't just drag me away with them, since I had made it clear I didn't belong to their religion. The average citizen saw me as a normal girl who just happened to receive the favor of the Goddess. Though they were respectful of me, they didn't go out of their way to give me any weird special treatment or anything — and that was just what I wanted. I don't know if you could call me a "normal girl" if I received the favor of the Goddess, though. Those with friends or family suffering from disease or other injuries might not have actually been so composed on the inside, but they couldn't try any funny business, since they knew trying to extort or pressure me meant calling down the wrath of the Goddess.

There may be some people out there who wanted to see me or come meet me in person when I was working as a salesperson, but unfortunately for them, I had nothing to do with the business side of the workshop. I just stayed in the back, doing stuff like cooking meals and cleaning up, which meant there wasn't any guarantee they'd see me if they tried paying a visit there. Even when I was out and about, everyone who knew me didn't seem to mind if the Goddess liked me or not. They saw me as me, and treated me the same as always. The same went with everyone else I met too, since it actually didn't seem like too many people realized who I was.

Though black hair wasn't a very common trait in this world, you could find quite a few other people with that hair color in a place as densely populated as the royal capital. Besides, the crowd that had gathered for that public Q&A session only represented a fraction of the people living in the capital, and an even smaller number of them had been close enough to see what I looked like. They didn't have photos here, either, so I didn't have to worry about my face being plastered all over the news by the media. The only thing people seemed to know about me was that I was a "girl with black hair." No one had seen my eye color or anything, so they didn't know what I looked like besides that.

So that's why I was here, casually strolling about town.

I didn't always just go to the marketplace or the library, or even to see the kids at the rundown house or anywhere like that. Sometimes I would just take walks by myself, and maybe do some shopping, or grab myself a bite to eat.

As I was busy stuffing my face with the meat skewers I had just bought from a food stall, I spotted a real stunner of a woman walking toward me. She looked young enough that I should probably call her a "girl," but any foreigner over fifteen looked like an adult in my eyes. You were considered an adult once you hit fifteen in this world, so maybe that wasn't too far off anyway...

She stood tall, cutting a rather gallant figure. She walked at a brisk pace and wore a sword on her waist. Judging from her garments, she looked to be a knight, or at least a knight-in-training.

As we were just about to walk by each other, the girl stopped dead in her tracks as she stared directly at my face. The expression on her own turned into one of shock before she cried out, "Oh my... Goddess!"

Well that *definitely sounds like the title of a certain long-running manga...*

"...Who are you again?"

I was a little confused by being called out by a girl I'd never seen before. The people around us seemed to think she'd just heard a distorted version of the rumors floating around, and paid us no mind.

"I-It's me! Francette, the knight!"

"...Again, *who*?"

That was the moment Francette realized she'd never even given the girl her name the last time they met. Even if she had, however, Kaoru probably would've forgotten it by now.

Things could have gotten complicated if Francette had kept calling Kaoru a goddess, so Kaoru dragged her off to a restaurant, since there weren't any cafes or coffee shops in this area.

There was still some time before lunch, so the inside of the shop was basically empty. The two sat down in a corner, where they wouldn't stand out, and each picked something random off the menu.

13

Kaoru asked again, "So... Who are you?"

Francette frantically began to explain everything.

She reminded Kaoru how they'd met in the forest, and how the potions Kaoru gave them had not only healed Hector and Yunith's grandmother, but also reminded her what had happened when she used the other two potions at the royal palace. Kaoru could only stare at her in blank amazement.

"So *that's* why the palace was so quick to spring into action... But, that aside..." Kaoru leaned over and stroked Francette's face. "I never would've thought it'd turn out *this* perfect... I guess that's what you get when you receive weird powers from a higher being who rivals God themself..."

"Uh... What?"

"Don't worry about it, it's nothing. Just talking to myself."

After trying to play that off, Kaoru sank deep into thought.

Well... Now what? Do I pretend like I'm not the "goddess" from before? Nah, that's probably a no-go... Even if my hair is a different color, my face is still exactly the same. Might be pushing it to say it's just a coincidence, too... It seems like she totally reveres me, so maybe if I play this off just right... Okay, let's do this!

"Francette, there's something I wish to ask of you."

"Y-Yes, of course! Please make use of me however you'd like!" Francette responded in a whisper, using the same hushed tone Kaoru had used.

There was plenty of distance between them and the other customers, but Kaoru kept her voice low as she explained her request.

"...And that's why I'm going around saying I'm Celestine's friend. To be honest, that isn't very far from the truth. All I'm doing is pretending to be a normal girl who... No, wait, that's not a lie, either. I've come down here in the form of a human, after all. I just happen to be a girl with some healing powers."

"I-I see…"

After what had happened to her, Francette had returned to the territory under Earl Adan's control, so as to get her personal affairs in order, and had only just made her way back to the capital a few days ago. She'd been living at an inn while she waited to be called back on duty at the royal palace, which was why she knew next to nothing about what had happened with Kaoru and the others in the central plaza.

"Anyway, I'm enjoying my life as a normal human girl, and I don't want anything getting in the way of that."

"O-Of course! I would never do anything to reveal your secret!" Francette swore, her back straight as an arrow.

"Oh, and while I appreciate you doing that, that's not exactly what I wanted to ask you…" Kaoru answered as she began explaining.

Though she was living a peaceful life at the moment, it was difficult for her to give her blessings out to the people with the way things were now. She wanted to become allies with someone who held some sway here. They had to be someone she could trust to protect her secret, and had enough power and influence to make sure they'd protect both themselves and Kaoru.

On that point, she was wondering if Francette could quietly put her into contact with the head of the household of the brother and sister she had met before. An earl should hold a pretty significant amount of power, and she'd already brought about a miracle for them with their grandmother—not to mention how the family and a good number of the king's ministers had borne witness to Francette's own miraculous transformation. Moreover, there was probably a much smaller chance of them trying to pull anything, compared to other nobles. She also didn't want to risk the chance of having to cut ties with any of her previously made relationships because it would otherwise put them in danger.

However…

"Oh, I've resigned my commission from Earl Adan. I've already moved out of his domain and transferred here to the capital…"

"Huh?"

Kaoru found herself dumbstruck once more when she found out the plan she'd just managed to put together was all for naught.

"…That is why, starting tomorrow, I will be in the employ of Roland, the king's brother, as his personal guard."

"What?!"

It looked like it was time for a change of plan…

That same time, at the royal palace—

"So our best course of action would be to reconcile with her, Roland?" King Serge asked his older brother.

"Right. We won't push our luck, and instead just do our best to win her over and gain her trust."

"Then let's have the Lyodart family handle this for now. After that, it's just a matter of using their influence to slowly expand the scope of people she'll speak with until it includes us. Should we raise Viscount Lyodart to the status of earl and assign him a post so the other nobles won't try to interfere?"

"Then he'd no longer be an 'unimportant' noble, right?" Roland replied with a shrug of his shoulders.

"Ah…"

Also at that same time, at the royal capital's main temple—

"So, should we be thinking of a way to bring her to our side, Archbishop?"

"Correct. We will slowly grow closer to her until the day comes where we can finally invite her to the temple," Archbishop Saulnier declared to Bishop Perrier. "She has already abandoned her home country, and she isn't in possession of friends or acquaintances who belong to the same religion as her. I should think it only be a matter of time before she joins us in worshiping Celestine with the Temple of the Goddess."

When he was finished, he turned toward the elderly oracle waiting patiently nearby.

"We shall be counting on you, Oracle Shaela. You are the one Goddess Celestine wished to speak to and deliver her divine revelation to the masses. I'm sure if anyone can earn the trust of a friend of the Goddess, it will be you. I shall have some others join you as well, so I leave it in your capable hands."

"Yes, you can leave it to me," Shaela respectfully answered.

Suddenly, a question popped into the archbishop's head and found itself being asked on his lips just as quickly as it had appeared.

"Incidentally, Shaela…it has already been over fifty years since you last spoke with the Goddess. Do you think you could share what you talked about with her back then? I couldn't help but wonder just what that could have been for these past fifty-three years, and I was hoping I might be able to know before I pass on, if at all possible…"

But the oracle only smiled and shook her head. "Not every word from the Goddess is a revelation for the masses, I'm afraid…"

"Is that so… Well, I already knew that was the answer I was going to get…" Archbishop Saulnier was smiling as he answered, but still seemed a little disappointed to hear it.

I can't say it! I can't just tell the archbishop that the only things we discussed were plans on how to get the attention of some guy she liked! That's all we did that whole time!

This was definitely a secret Shaela knew she had to take with her to her grave...

Back at the Maillart Workshop—

Everyone there was treating Kaoru just about the same as they usually did. All they asked from her was to help cook and clean. They weren't trying to use her to get in the Goddess's good graces, as they were more than happy just having a cute girl there with them. After all, it wasn't like the Goddess herself would come down to help them cook and clean, or come help with the metalwork in the shop, or anything like that.

Today, another member of the temple had come to pay a visit to the workshop. The oracle Shaela came every day to invite Kaoru to come to the temple so they could chat, and every day Kaoru refused, on the grounds that she didn't want to go to any temple that was of a different religion than her own. This time, Shaela had come with the suggestion that they meet at a restaurant instead. When Kaoru looked into the restaurant in question, she discovered that it was supposed to have a completely soundproof room way in the back...

A shiver ran through Kaoru's body, and she immediately shot down that particular idea.

The next time she heard from Shaela, it was to ask if she'd like to meet in a place of her choosing. Kaoru figured Shaela wasn't going to give up until the oracle got a chance to see her again, so she resigned herself to visiting with the older woman—but not in any secret back rooms or anything. She wanted to meet in a place where everyone could see them.

18

A few days later, at a certain restaurant—

Kaoru had found some free time between cleaning up after making lunch at the workshop and getting ready to make dinner. She set aside some of that time to finally give in and meet up with Shaela.

"My apologies for keeping you waiting."

The oracle in question had appeared, along with an assortment of boys and girls following after her. There were five of them total, three boys and two girls, spanning anywhere from ten to sixteen years old, each one of them more handsome or beautiful than the last.

A long, drawn-out sigh escaped Kaoru's lips.

"These are some of the children who are studying at the temple. When they heard I was coming to meet with you, they *insisted* on coming along as well..." Shaela explained as she took a seat, a smile playing on her lips.

"Right, sure..." Kaoru gave a listless reply. "So, why did you want to see me?"

Shaela panicked slightly after seeing that Kaoru had zero interest in the kids, switching the conversation to something they shared common ground on: Celestine.

"So, Kaoru...did Lady Celestine, erm...say anything about the other God she wanted to get along with?"

Though it was in front of the children, this was the only conversation she could bring up to talk to Kaoru about. She was hoping it would make Kaoru think Celestine was a close friend of hers as well.

"What, Celes talked to you about that, too? Yeah, she seemed pretty happy about having a chance to talk with him."

"Ah, really? That's wonderful news!" Even though she was the one to bring it up, Shaela was shocked to learn that things were actually going well for the Goddess.

Did the plans I thought up for her end up working?

"…"

But Kaoru added nothing further to the conversation.

On to the next topic then…

"Regarding the statue of Lady Celestine you asked about before… It was decided when it was commissioned, since she's the Goddess who brings about abundant crops, it seemed more natural to give her a more abundant figure to match. That's why they didn't want her to seem so pitifully flat…"

"…I see," came Kaoru's frigid reply.

Shaela's gaze dropped to Kaoru's chest, which was the exact moment she realized the horrible, horrible mistake she'd just made.

Pitifully flat… Pitifully flat… Pitifully flat…

Shaela began sweating as the silence stretched out between them.

"W-Well, um, let me introduce you to the children. Starting from the left—"

"No need. I won't be able to remember them anyway."

"Oh…" Shaela was at a loss for words.

She shot down my foolproof plan with the kids! I was hoping to switch the conversation to them if I ever got in trouble, but now I don't have that option anymore… It's still too soon to bring up going to the temple, since I can't be too upfront about it. I have to at least try and warm her up a bit more with some normal conversation first…

That's when the children came to her rescue.

"We wanna hear about what the Goddess is like!"

"Oh, me too!"

"I wanna hear about her as well!"

Well, I can certainly see why the archbishop chose these kids. Their looks aren't the only good thing about them, it seems, Shaela thought to herself, impressed.

Kaoru turned toward the kids. "All right, listen. Let's pretend that you guys had a super rich friend."

"Huh?"

"What would you think about people who came chasing after you just to ask you about your rich friend instead of you? Do you think they'd make good friends? Would you even *want* to be friends with them? And while we're on the subject, do you think you would trust someone who'd just blab about their friend to a complete stranger?"

"..."

"Well, since it looks like we don't have anything to talk about, I'll be taking my leave now," Kaoru said as she stood up from her seat. Shaela and the kids stayed silent, not moving a muscle.

It was only after she left the restaurant that Kaoru realized something: "Oh... I didn't even order anything, huh."

A few days later, Francette came around to the workshop.

"Kaoru, Earl Adan's family has arrived in the capital."

That was exactly the news Kaoru had been waiting for. She made sure to confirm they'd be meeting tomorrow, right after lunch. She'd also made sure to tell Francette and the others not to call her "Goddess," an "angel," or even a "friend of the Goddess."

21

The next day, Kaoru had elected to wear the hand-me-downs she'd "borrowed" from Baron Renie's daughter as she stood in front of the residence Earl Adan owned in the royal capital. It gave her that "daughter of a poor, lower-class noble family" look, which was just what she was going for—although no matter how low-ranking she was supposed to be, a noble girl would almost never be out walking around by themselves.

After using the knocker on the door to announce herself, she was shown inside by a steward, who proceeded to guide her to a room deeper in the house.

She had her pepper spray handy, just in case anything happened, but she had a backup plan as well: In the event that she didn't emerge of the earl's mansion by sundown, she'd already given instructions to the children of the Eyes of the Goddess to send word to the temple, Viscount Lyodart, and the workshop, that she'd been captured by a noble, and to cause a commotion by shouting that loudly in the central plaza. That was the only time they could go out of their way to call her "the Goddess's friend." Just using the name "Kaoru" wouldn't have much of an impact, since people weren't all that familiar with her under that name. She wasn't all that worried about any of that coming to pass though.

By the time Kaoru arrived in the room, all the other members of this meeting were already gathered there: Earl Adan; his son, Hector; his daughter, Yunith; the captain of his envoy of knights, Robert; Francette; and the king's brother, Roland.

All right, time to get plotting...

There was nothing Kaoru enjoyed more than putting a good plot together.

There was a chance that some people in this room would realize she was the same person as the silver-haired goddess they'd met in the forest, while others had been healed or had their family members healed by her blessings. Basically, it was a gathering of people she was worried about being left alone too long, as well as people she knew would have an almost zero percent chance of betraying her.

Kaoru explained everything to the group as follows:

She was a friend of Celes, who had come here from another world because Celes suggested that she do so herself, and had taken on the form of a human to make that request. That was all a secret, so she wanted them to keep that on the down-low. Right now, she was just pretending to be a normal human who had some healing powers, thanks to being friends with the Goddess, making sure to put aside how any of that made her even a remotely normal human being.

She made clear she had no intention of backing someone in power, either. However, though she only wanted to grace the people with some of her blessings, it had become much harder to do so after all the commotion from earlier. So, for that reason, it wasn't like she wouldn't consider doing so...to a certain degree, that is.

After much deliberation among the group, they decided upon a number of things: the only official point of contact she would allow the royal family, the various aristocrats, or the people from the temple to speak with her through would be the Lyodart household. The viscount and his family only knew of the public image she'd established, so there wouldn't be any changes with them. The *un*official channels, on the other hand, would be through the Adan household, or Roland, with communications between him and Kaoru delivered via Francette.

At Roland's request, no one else was to know the truth besides the king. It would be harder for them to move around freely if they didn't at least tell him, since it might otherwise spark suspicions of them plotting a rebellion or something of the sort. Roland had already turned down the throne once, so there wasn't any need to worry about that, but it was better to play it safe here. You could still find people with rocks for brains among the nobility and royal family, after all.

At Francette's rather insistent urging, a name was given to the group of people gathered here: *The Light of the Goddess*. Kaoru protested vehemently, but since Francette, Roland, and even Hector and Yunith agreed on the name, it passed according to majority rule.

And so, they officially began their operations.

The first order of business regarded the sale of healing potions. They would be sold at affordable prices, but would only have limited effects, which would expire if they weren't used within five days. How they were produced and circulated would be a national secret, and the royal palace would act as the distributor.

The five-day expiration date was to prevent people from buying them all up or stockpiling them for use in times of war. The most beneficial thing they could be used for was to heal injured hunters or soldiers, and cure anyone else who fell ill. Since they wouldn't be that strong, they wouldn't be able to heal old wounds or scars that had already healed, but they should still be plenty useful enough for the common citizen.

Any true miracle would call for the "tears of the goddess," which, as the name suggested, had to be created with the power of a goddess. The healing potions were Kaoru's way of saying that, while someone may not be worthy of receiving the blessing of the Goddess, they could at least receive a drop of her mercy in the form of a potion.

Kaoru then remembered a couple other things she wanted to bring up with everyone.

First off, the Light of the Goddess had an outside group working alongside them: the Eyes of the Goddess. Though they were working for free at the moment, she announced that she had plans to bring them on as formal members and provide them with proper salaries. As for item number two, they would be using the Abili Trade Company to handle the trade routes for the potions.

And with that, Kaoru had finally managed to find a way to begin selling her potions.

"Excuse me! Is Kaoru here?"

Francette had shown up again at the workshop, but this time a bit flustered.

"What's wrong? The potions shouldn't be going on sale for a while, right?"

"N-No, this is about something else. A diplomat from a neighboring country arrived here yesterday…"

I had a bad feeling as soon as I heard that. I mean, with four countries next to this one, it couldn't possibly be…

"From *which* country, exactly?"

"The Kingdom of Brancott."

Aghhh, I knew it! My head drooped as far as I could let it.

"So that diplomat you were talking about…"

"Believe it or not, I heard it's the crown prince himself, of all people!"

Ahhhhhh…

There was no way the prince and whoever else had come with him were going to do much in the way of being "diplomats." It seemed more likely that they'd barged in, declaring that they'd heard a girl named Kaoru had arrived here from their country, and asked to meet with her, probably causing serious headaches for the king and his ministers in the process. They most likely couldn't just flat out refuse the crown prince of one of their neighboring countries, but they also couldn't let him meet with me without knowing why he wanted to do so.

But there were still plenty of people who knew where to find me. There was a chance that someone was either trying to get closer to the prince, or was hoping to start something with the prince of another country, and would tell him where I was. That was why Francette had come here to warn me, on Roland's orders.

"...Right. Dealing with them is gonna be a pain, so let's get them to go back as soon as humanly possible. We'll tell them to meet us at the Lyodart household since I don't want to trouble everyone at the workshop. I'll leave it to them to decide when we meet, but make sure it's after lunch, please."

I couldn't just skip out on making lunch for the workshop; it was my job, after all.

"Understood. I will pass that along to Sir Roland."

After hearing what I had to say, Francette took her leave.

It was that evening when I heard from the Lyodart household that my audience with the prince would be held just two days later.

Prince Fernand was in high spirits. Not only was he finally going to see Kaoru, but she had apparently declared that she'd never come to the royal palace. Instead, they'd be meeting at the residence of some unimportant-sounding viscount. It seemed like the temple wasn't even going to be involved at all.

"If the only ally she's found here is a mere viscount, I'm sure they'll hand her over if we pressure them hard enough."

"That all depends on what *Kaoru* wants, not the viscount. Don't forget what happened last time, Fernand," Fabio warned him.

"Ngh… I suppose you're right…"

Though he was the one who had given the warning, even Fabio didn't think what Fernand suggested was totally out of the question. From what they'd had their subordinates dig up, it sounded like Kaoru had become quite infamous throughout this country. It must be difficult for her to live any semblance of a normal life here. The only story of her that had spread in Brancott was that she was a girl devoted to the prince, but the details of what had actually happened were known only among the nobility…mostly because the verbal thrashing Kaoru had given him would be considered disrespectful.

Since her name and appearance were being kept secret there, no one would connect the girl named Kaoru, who had been working at the restaurant, with the same girl covered in blood from the night of the party. That's why everyone would think she was an entirely different person, meaning she'd be able to live a normal life back in their capital. The only problem was if this country would allow them to take her back.

According to the other diplomatic envoys they'd sent out before coming here, no one from the country had even attempted to make a move to get her. It wasn't that they didn't have an interest in Kaoru, but that they just couldn't do anything to her. Just having Kaoru in their country would be a boon, especially since she'd received the favor of the Goddess. Having the blessing of the Goddess was one thing, but with her knowledge, it couldn't be overstated how much of an asset she'd be if the royal family could just get on her good side.

How much of that did the royalty and upper echelons of this country already realize? Just what sort of importance did they place on Kaoru, when compared to the crown prince of Brancott?

Fabio couldn't quite get a read on that.

"At any rate, we should avoid being too overbearing or saying anything rude. We'll take things slow, being as amiable as possible, to try and win her over. First, we'll ask her what her situation is like here, then we apologize for what happened before and offer her our assistance. In the end, *she* has to be the one to say she'll return to Brancott."

"All right." Fernand nodded in response. "We'll go with that."

Two days later—

Fernand, Fabio, and Allan were accompanied to the residence of Viscount Lyodart by Roland and Prime Minister Corneau, protected by an entourage of guards. There was no need to use the knocker when they arrived, of course, since their welcome committee was already lined up outside the viscount's residence to meet them.

Usually, it would only be natural for the viscount to come and greet him in person, considering the prince's status. However, it was the prince who was coming to visit the viscount, so the viscount was waiting to receive him inside his manor instead.

Leaving several guards posted in front of the mansion and in the entranceway, the group was led further inside. Once they arrived in the reception room, they found Viscount Lyodart and his third-oldest son, Achille, waiting for them there.

After sitting down and exchanging the briefest of greetings, Fernand was quick in asking to meet with Kaoru. Acknowledging his request, the viscount gave an order to one of his servants. The doors to the room opened, and in walked a single girl.

"Kaoru!!!" the three shouted as they jumped up from their seats.

"Wh-What happened to the injury on your face?"

"Thank goodness you're all right…"

The girl stared back at them blankly before a sudden look of realization crossed her face.

"Oh, you all know my little sister!"

"Huh?"

"My name is Alfa Kaoru Nagase. It sounds like you've already met my little sister, *Mifa* Kaoru Nagase."

"WHAAAAAAT?!"

"Oh dear, did she not mention me? They sent people after us right as we fled our home country, which is why we split up and went our separate ways. I was hoping we'd meet again someday, but who would have thought she'd settled down in the country right next to me… Is she doing all right?" Kaoru asked back, glossing over entirely what they had said about injuries and her being all right.

"W-Well, um…"

The three didn't know how to respond. They couldn't just say how she'd injured herself and then suddenly went missing.

"Would one of those two over there be her *special* man?"

Shock was the only word to describe the look on Allan and Fabio's faces as she said that.

"Wait, why them?!" Fernand balked, seemingly unable to comprehend what she just said.

"They're both her type: strong, bold men who look like they have some integrity to them. They also seem kind, with good heads on their shoulders. They're the type of people she'd enjoy talking with. They also seem like guys who'll become even more ruggedly handsome with age."

"B-But, I'm—"

"She's always hated self-centered, flashy guys who only care about themselves, *especially* ones who look like age will get the better of them."

Fernand fell into shocked silence at her words, while Allan and Fabio could only send looks of pity his way.

"Then, if you don't mind me asking, can Mifa also use the Goddess's healing power?"

'Alfa' Kaoru shook her head in response.

"No, I'm the only one who has befriended Celes. Do you think she picks her friends by how they look, perhaps? Even if we look alike, my sister and I are completely different. We ran away from our country because we were both being targeted: me for my healing powers, and she for her vast knowledge and talent. But this is quite the predicament…" Kaoru mused aloud. "I came here in the hopes of making this country more prosperous, but it looks like she's going to beat me to the punch if she's been in the country right next to me this whole time…"

The three men grimaced in unison at her words.

"Then how about you come to the Kingdom of Brancott as well, Alfa? You could live together with your little sister!" Fabio insisted.

"I'm afraid that won't work," Kaoru replied, shaking her head at his invitation. "We'd only upset the balance of both countries if we stayed in the same one together. Doing so would lead to all sorts of quarrels and disputes, and I don't want to have to flee for my life again because of it. Besides, I'm sure I'll have another chance to see her again someday."

"…"

If this girl claimed to be someone different from Kaoru, then they didn't have any reason to take her back to Brancott with them. Neither the viscount nor Balmore would be thrilled to hear that they wanted to steal away a girl they'd only just met—a highly valuable girl at that.

There was nothing more for them to talk about. In low spirits, Fernand and the others put the Lyodart residence behind them...

"...Do you really think they're sisters?" Allan asked.

"It doesn't matter if that was her big sister, or just Kaoru herself..." Fabio responded, a sober expression on his face. "The only thing that *is* certain is that she has not even the slightest interest in Fernand or in coming back to Brancott."

Despair clouded Fernand's face at those words.

Allan and Fabio couldn't help but wonder what could have been if they hadn't brought Fernand to the restaurant that day. If it had just been the two of them, and if they'd managed to get closer to her little by little, then... Alas, it was far too late to think about such trivialities now.

"Whew, thank goodness *that's* over with! They shouldn't come around bothering me anymore after all that!" Kaoru remarked, looking refreshed as she took a big stretch. Everyone else, on the other hand, didn't look quite as renewed as her.

"So...would that person you mentioned actually happen to be your sister...?" Everyone already knew the answer, but Francette still thought she should ask, just in case.

"Of course not! C'mon, this is *me* we're talking about! You already know me well enough, so you shouldn't even need to ask that!"

Yeah, that figures... everyone thought.

Even if it were in jest, all those present had been cringing at Kaoru's behavior toward the prince.

Chapter 9:
War

At last, the potion-selling business that Kaoru had always wanted to start up had finally begun taking shape. As the effects of what her potions could do began spreading around the rumor mill, the market for them opened in a flash.

The Abili Trade Company acted as the distributor, sending their main inventory to their branch stores in other towns and consigning smaller stock to local shops where Abili hadn't operated.

Those who lived somewhere five or more days outside of the shipping territories would need to travel to a town close enough to get the potions before the expiration date kicked in. Considering this, however, it wasn't all that much to ask to fix any injury or sickness that ailed them. They didn't even have to go all the way to the capital. There were also express horses sent out every day to reach those too infirm to move properly or those who required immediate aid. They even traveled to the poorer areas, and the fastest horses could reach almost any destination in the country within four days.

As you can imagine, there were plenty of aristocrats, moneybags, government officials, and soldiers who would be willing to fork over the cash to keep the horses running, just in case anything happened. If nothing did occur and they didn't need such aid after all, they'd be able to sell off the extra potions for cheap to the public, since the potions would lose its effectiveness the day after being delivered.

All deliveries made by express horse went through strict regulations: Could the person in question really not make it to one of the other towns selling potions? Was there any chance of them just being in it to trying to sell the potions off to someone else?

If it was ever discovered the recipient was illegally reselling the potions or they were guilty of some other crime, the perpetrator's family, relatives, even their friends and acquaintances, would lose the privilege of receiving potions. Such a ban would stay in effect for the perpetrator's lifetime, which would usually result in the perpetrator being murdered by one of their relatives.

If it turned out to be a noble trying to twist the distribution of potions in their favor, they'd no longer receive shipments to the territories they controlled—also for the duration of their lifetime. Strangely enough, those types of nobles usually ended up dead after a horrible accident befell them or after succumbing to a mysterious illness, which would be when their sons would take over as heads of household.

It went without saying that the nobles who were more decent human beings and shared their potions with the masses experienced an upswell of goodwill.

The youths with promising futures who had been cruelly taken away due to minor negligence were dwindling in number. Soldiers could devote themselves fully to their training and duties without concern for injuries, leading to major improvements in their abilities and skills.

The people of the royal capital could all probably guess where the potions were coming from, but they didn't dare pry into the matter. No one thought they could glean any benefit from trying to get involved. If they did, and things went south, it could mean losing the potions for good. Since they'd have to bear the entirety of the blame for such a grievous crime, they had a pretty good reason to keep to themselves—besides, they thought poking their noses where they didn't belong would earn them a visit from the castle's soldiers.

The number of sick and injured people in the Kingdom of Balmore gradually declined; meanwhile, the birth rate was on the rise. With the previously sick and disabled able to return to work, the budget and personnel needed to run care facilities or provide medicine for individuals like them were on the decline as well.

However, Kaoru was sure to warn them, given that something might happen to her, that they still needed to train people as doctors and other medical professions that required substantial training ahead of time. They had to keep improving their own medical techniques, as well as preparing an appropriate budget and other necessary arrangements, should the worst come to pass. She had Roland make sure the king understood that, loud and clear.

Since the capital of Grua lay slightly farther to the east, it took about six days by cart for potions to reach the border between Brancott and Balmore, or around two to three days by express horse. Because Aras, the capital of Brancott, lay further to the west, potions could be delivered there if they sent a professional rider on horseback. That way, the Kingdom of Brancott was just barely able to receive the prosperity brought by potions, as well.

Balmore had strong, long-established ties with the Kingdom of Aseed to the south, so they could stand in solidarity against the militaristic Aligot Empire that lay to the west of the two countries. Because they had the good fortune of sharing their northern and southern borders with each other, Aseed was also able to receive the blessing of potions.

The northernmost parts of Balmore faced the ocean, which stretched all the way from the northeast of the country to the center of the northern border.

To the northwest lay the Holy Land of Rueda, a country roughly one-tenth of the size of Balmore. It was a theocratic nation, formed long ago around the area where the Goddess Celestine had descended from on high to save the people. Though it was a small country, other countries still paid their due respects to Rueda.

But with the goddess not showing herself over the past fifty-three years, the number of pilgrimages had declined, which meant the amount of offerings the country received had drastically fallen, as well. Fishing was the only industry available to them, outside of their religious influence, and they were slowly losing power as a country.

With rumors spreading about the "miracles of the Goddess" happening in Balmore, Rueda gave the order to have the angel bringing about those miracles brought before them. However, the archbishop of the main temple in the capital replied that they couldn't do so because she wasn't of the same faith as them, while the only response they received from the king was how they couldn't comply because Balmore kept religious and governmental affairs separate.

Then came the circulation of the healing potions. After sending their own people to investigate, it was deemed that it was as if the distributors had bottled a fragment of miraculous prowess from the Goddess herself. And the source of those potions: the Kingdom of Balmore.

Rueda believed that it was the only place that should be blessed with miracles. At this rate, Balmore would steal away their "holy land" title.

With the sense of impending danger weighing all the more heavily on the top brass of Rueda, the country began concocting a variety of schemes to deal with the situation unfolding before them.

At the very edge of the peninsula, which was home to all these countries, was the Aligot Empire, a country that focused all of its efforts on strengthening its military might. It shared its borders with the Holy Land of Rueda in the north, the Kingdom of Aseed in the south, and even the Kingdom of Balmore along its central borders. Steep mountains stood between it and the other countries, however, which meant the only way to travel by cart was along the northern coastline to Rueda, or the southern one to Aseed. If anyone from Aligot wanted to head directly to Balmore, they would have to traverse the treacherous mountains on foot without the aid of horses.

Aligot didn't have much in the way of industry going for it, and the three countries that bordered the empire were able to extract the same resources from the oceans and mountains. This was why the other three countries didn't feel like they had to force themselves to trade with Aligot, or set their sights on trying to claim their land for themselves.

But the same couldn't be said of the Aligot Empire. To accommodate the growth of its own country, it needed to keep expanding toward the main portion of the peninsula. If it couldn't gain any new territory from across the mountain range, it wouldn't be able to meet the needs of its country with what it produced on its own. That was why it poured so much of its national spending into developing its military.

A country that barely saw trade and concentrated all its resources to strengthen its military... The only choice available was to put that military might to use, and soon.

It was then that the Kingdom of Balmore began saturating the market with potions. By some cruel twist of fate, the potions only worked within five days of making them. Even if the empire tried importing them via Rueda, the potions wouldn't make it to Aligot before their expiration date was up.

That meant they couldn't be used for war!

But if the potions couldn't be delivered within five days, then Aligot needed to make its own potions. That way it could use all the potions it wanted to conduct its military campaigns. It would force the other countries to surrender to its overwhelming military might, and it would finally be able to expand into the main continent!

To make that happen, Aligot had to bring down the Kingdom of Balmore and obtain the secret of making those potions for itself.

Thus marked the beginning of the Aligot Empire putting its plans into action…

"So that makes five, then…"

"Indeed. That would make three incidents from Rueda, and two from Aligot, thus far," the prime minister said, recapping the current state of affairs to the king while Roland stood at Serge's side.

"Requests to be put into contact with Kaoru, invitations for her to go to their country, and even attempted kidnappings…"

"Fortunately for us, the spies Miss Kaoru has been turning in to us have related everything they know. Since we've already captured those responsible for sending reports back detailing the events after making contact with her, I would think the countries that sent them shouldn't have received any information about her."

"But there must be other spies out there besides the group trying to contact Kaoru directly and the team supporting them. Even if they don't report back on what happened after making contact with her, they should already know about Kaoru herself. She's fairly well-known around the capital, after all..."

"I know we expected Aligot to make their move soon, but I never thought Rueda would resort to taking extreme measures like these, as well..." Roland spoke up, adding to the discussion. "Are they not afraid of rousing the Goddess's anger, or having divine punishment dropped on their heads? Even if they *did* capture Kaoru, they must have known it'd be practically impossible to force her to do as they wished."

"Perhaps they only think of Miss Kaoru as a girl who can make potions?" the prime minister suggested.

"Huh...?" Serge and Roland exchanged glances.

"At any rate, we can assume the empire will begin their invasion soon enough. Now it's only a matter of whether they will occupy Aseed before leading an assault on our country, forcing their way through Aseed to attack us directly, or if they will pass through Rueda to get to us, since the Holy Land is neutral territory..."

"But Rueda would never allow Aligot's armies to pass through, correct? Their neutrality wouldn't allow such a thing."

"The question then is if a country backed into a corner would actually respect something like that."

"You're right..."

"At any rate, we need to send a messenger to Rueda to warn them of Aligot's plans, and to request that they contact us should anything happen. Let's dispatch guards from our own country there as well. After that, all that's left is for us to increase our defenses so that the soldiers are ready to move out at any time."

"Right, that's just about all we can do..." Roland agreed.

At that very moment, the sound of frantic footsteps rapidly drew closer toward them...

Potion sales were booming. Kaoru didn't really want to become filthy rich off the potion business, but it was true that the more money she had meant the more things she could do.

The first thing Kaoru did was rent a nice house with a garden on the edge of the commoners' district. It was a bit worn down, but still a fairly large place—large enough that she had all the members of the Eyes of the Goddess stay there, as well.

After getting them all proper sets of nice clothes to wear, she did her best getting them some normal work: waiting jobs at restaurants, doing odd jobs for people about town, working food carts in the plaza… There were all sorts of jobs they could do that made it easier to gather information.

The food carts did a roaring trade selling the pseudo-takoyaki, taiyaki, and udon that Kaoru had come up with. Kaoru's friends at the workshop had made the molds for the takoyaki and taiyaki, and she'd made sure to pay them for the job, of course.

Besides the potion business, Kaoru was also continuing to distribute her magical cure-all tears of the goddess in secret…but to be honest, it was a pretty public secret at this point. Everyone always had the same reaction when she showed up wearing her mask: They would act surprised for her benefit and exclaim things like, "Wh-Who are you?!" always making sure to say things like, "I don't know who you are, but thank you!" when she left.

Much to Emile's (and everyone else's) shock, Kaoru was actually under the impression that no one knew it was her. But no one was going to be fooled by just a mask, and that went double if they already knew her. That kind of stuff only happened in the magical girl shows Kaoru watched as a kid in her world.

That was how Kaoru had earned the gratitude and goodwill of the people, thus guaranteeing that no noble or anyone from the temple would be able to lay a finger on her without some sort of retribution. Kaoru's place in the kingdom was all but assured.

Every once in awhile she'd have to deal with strange people trying to get close to her, but they would always spill their guts and reveal their true plans after drinking some of the tea she served them. That was when she'd give a signal to the plainclothes guards (probably assigned to watch over her) who would come and take them away.

Kaoru had no interest whatsoever in getting involved with some militaristic country, much less a religious state. But, unbeknownst to her, the situation between these countries was changing far more rapidly than she could have ever possibly imagined.

"Your Majesty, the empire has made their move!" the soldier exclaimed as he burst into the room.

"What?! Where are they invading from, Rueda or Aseed?!"

"Th-They..." The soldier hesitated slightly before answering the king. "They came through the mountains! They're advancing directly on Balmore!"

"Oh, no..."

Disbelief escaped the lips of the king and his ministers. Had heavily armed soldiers actually made it through such a forbidding mountain path? How would they receive any supplies if not even wagons could traverse the treacherous route? The questions were endless, but there was no use worrying about them now, if they had indeed already made it over the mountains.

"What are their forces like?"

"Approximately 30,000, sir. It appears just under 10,000 of them are transportation personnel, and half of those are retreating back through the mountains. The remaining 5,000 are said to be dragging carts they've assembled after crossing the mountain range."

"So they sent back the people they didn't need after they finished carrying the weapons and disassembled carts... That means we must be looking at around 20,000 soldiers and 5,000 transport troops..."

They immediately launched into an emergency meeting to decide how to handle the sudden developments before them. Though the Kingdom of Balmore stretched from east to west, the royal capital of Grua lay more on the eastern side. Aligot was invading through the western edge of the country, the farthest spot from the capital. There was still plenty of time, but the longer they took to respond, the greater the damage the western towns would take. With the invading forces lacking supplies, it was expected that the usual process of ransacking homes and commandeering goods would be that much more ruthless as a result.

Balmore had 40,000 soldiers and 4,000 support troops available for its counterattack. Since the conflict was happening inside the kingdom, Balmore held the advantage when it came to supplying its troops. They could actually use horses, unlike their enemy, and in terms of pure military strength, they had double the soldiers of the Aligot forces, all of whom were ready to deploy almost immediately.

However, the emphasis was on "almost." These weren't exactly the armies you would find back on modern-day Earth, and it would take a few days to gather the resources necessary to send out the troops.

"No mounted troops, and 20,000 soldiers... Do they think they can win with just that?" one of the ministers murmured.

"No, there may be another two or three waves of reinforcements still crossing the mountains. Half of their transport troops turned back, after all..."

"True. They may not be preparing for a direct assault on the capital, but planning to build up a stronghold by occupying the western territories before slowly advancing on Grua. There's also the possibility that they could throw something simple together using the carts and wagons they seize from the territories they invade."

"In any case, we should be thankful to have Brancott at our backs. We'll be able to send all our forces west without worrying about what's behind us. Brancott and Aseed should both know that Aligot will come for them next if we fall, so it's impossible to think they would betray us."

"Yes, we can be sure of that, at least."

The meeting continued after deciding what course of action to take. The person in charge of logistics ran off to put out a call for soldiers and to prepare wagons and supplies for the battle ahead.

And so, the war raged on.

There was no open declaration of hostilities, yet the army of one country had invaded through another's borders. It was plain to see they were already at war.

The royal capital was abuzz with talk about it, but no one seemed to have a particularly grim outlook on the matter. It was common knowledge that the Aligot Empire devoted most of its efforts into strengthening its military, but it didn't have much in the way of national finance due to the steep mountains that half-isolated the country. Even its population was smaller compared to the other countries around it. Not only that, but crossing the mountains to invade meant that the soldiers couldn't bring horses or any significant quantity of weapons with them, so it wouldn't even be able to put the full might of its military to good use.

There was still a great distance between them and the royal capital. Even if, by some chance, the enemy succeeded in their advance, there was plenty of time for its citizens to escape. So long as people weren't around when the actual fighting broke out, they wouldn't have to fear for their lives.

Now, it wasn't as if the soldiers were all bloodthirsty conquerors who wanted to massacre everyone in the territories they would occupy or anything like that. The invading forces would just treat the people living there as new citizens to collect revenue from. To the residents, it would just seem like they changed tax collectors...so long as their occupiers didn't ransack them first, that is.

Just days after learning of the enemy's plans, the allied soldiers who had gathered from the surrounding nobles' territories joined with the main forces in the royal capital before heading out to battle. They would rendezvous with the other troops out on the western front as they advanced on the encroaching army. The question that remained was whether they would meet the enemy while en route, or if they would have to break through the simple fortified encampments the enemy soldiers had thrown together.

It took time relaying messages in this world, so it was nearly impossible to get an accurate read on what the enemy was doing. Generals were in charge of giving orders to the soldiers on the field, while the king himself would never show up on the front lines. All he had to do was keep himself heavily fortified in the royal castle. If they were to lose the war, however, he would be the one to offer himself up over the lives of the people. That was his job, and the price he paid for the immense power he held.

It had been seven days since the armies left the royal capital to intercept the invading forces. King Serge and his brother Roland were currently in the middle of a meeting with their ministers.

"Considering how many days it took for news of the enemy's invasion to reach us, the days needed to prepare our soldiers, and the week since we sent out our army...if the enemy didn't elect to stay put, our forces should be making contact with them right about now," the king murmured to himself.

"Yes, that's correct," one of the king's advisors responded. "The enemy should be moving at a snail's pace due to their lack of horses. Even if our forces are avoiding forced marches to prevent exhausting our soldiers, it should only be a matter of time."

"But it will still take several days for us to know even that…"

Considering the time it took for them to send out their forces, it should have taken the soldiers around six to seven days to finally engage with the enemy. But as it was, there was no way for them to know if that was true or not, at least not right now.

The battlefield for this skirmish was far removed from the Aligot Empire's borders. Even if they used the fastest horses they had, its army still had to deal with the mountain range that separated the empire from everything else. It would take at least ten days before Aligot heard any news about when the fighting had started.

Just as they were about to wrap up the meeting, a messenger came rushing into the room.

"Urgent news! Aligot forces have invaded Balmore through Rueda's borders, around 20,000 strong!"

"WHAT?!"

The meeting room was in an uproar. It wasn't that they hadn't considered the possibility of Aligot invading on multiple fronts, since that was exactly why they'd kept soldiers behind to protect the royal capital. More troops from the easternmost corners of Balmore hadn't arrived in time to head out with the main force, so the extra soldiers were stationed around the capital to bolster their forces near Grua. All together, their numbers totaled around 15,000, less than the soldiers advancing upon them from Rueda.

Having fewer soldiers wouldn't be so much of a problem if they were going to be fighting a defensive battle. They'd be in a tight spot if the enemy outnumbered them more than three-to-one, but they should still hold the advantage if it was 20,000 against 15,000. Even then, however, that would mean they'd have to hole up in the capital and fight using siege warfare tactics in order for them to have a chance at winning. If it came down to that, all the towns in the enemy's path would fall victim to looting and pillaging, and trying to fight a long, drawn-out siege would lead to the soldiers taking all sorts of losses as well.

Adding more to the pile of issues they already had to deal with, the new problem was the possibility that Rueda had become their enemy as well. The only way Aligot's forces could invade Rueda was through the northwestern coastline, which meant that Rueda should have been able to send a report to Balmore about the invading forces immediately.

With Rueda's neutrality trampled on, Rueda should have done everything it could to stop Aligot while requesting aid from the other countries—and yet, Balmore had received no such request.

Only one conclusion could be drawn from that realization: Rueda had aligned itself with the Aligot Empire.

"Any orders we send to our main forces now won't make it in time. Even if they manage to repel the enemy in front of them, they'll end up taking massive losses if they're attacked from behind. Our only choice now is to send a messenger to let them know of the situation and have them come back immediately after fending off the enemy forces they're currently dealing with. We will wall ourselves off in the capital and have our main forces attack them from the rear when they return."

"But if their goal is to distract our main forces so their armies can simply avoid fighting and retreat, this conflict will never get resolved, wouldn't you agree?"

The ministers all voiced their opinions one after the other. They all made valid points, but the choices currently available to them were limited.

In the end, they decided upon reporting the situation to their main forces and ordering a retreat, then having the soldiers in the capital prepare for siege warfare.

The next day, an envoy from Rueda arrived at the palace. They presented themselves as a cardinal, riding in an extravagant coach along with their attendants. They came bearing a handwritten letter from the pope, expressing his desire to take the girl who received the blessing of the Goddess under his care before the city was engulfed in war.

It was all one grand farce, and the king and everyone else knew it. The ministers firmly expressed their desire to reject him and show the cardinal the door, but Roland had other plans.

"No, let's have them meet with Kaoru and have *her* persuade them instead."

The ministers were shocked, vehemently voicing their opposition to the idea. King Serge, on the other hand, knew his brother well, and, for some reason, a smile was playing on his lips.

"But," Roland continued, "that's only after we make sure to explain *precisely* what's going on to her—and you can be sure we'll tell her *everything*."

As the ministers thought back on what Kaoru had done and the verbal thrashings she had given in the past, grins slowly crept across their features. It was unanimously decided that they would go along with Roland's proposition.

After receiving a message from Francette, Kaoru found herself going to the Adan residence for the first time in a while. That they weren't meeting at the Lyodart household meant that this wasn't a public gathering.

When she arrived, Roland proceeded to fill her in on all sorts of things: the situation between the countries, how the empire had been driven into a corner, the war, and even what Rueda had been plotting.

"So does that mean...this war is my fault?" Kaoru asked Roland.

"No, it's not," came his ready reply. "From a geopolitical standpoint, Aligot *had* to invade another country due to being trapped in their corner of the peninsula. They then focused too much on developing their military power on top of that. Wars aren't something you can be ready for with just a few months of preparation, after all, which is exactly why they've been preparing all this time. At most, they may have just decided to include you on their long list of reasons for starting this war."

Kaoru was a little relieved to hear Roland say that. The thought of someone starting a war over her had twisted her stomach in knots... But more than that, she was pissed about what Rueda was doing.

"Alright, I got it," Kaoru answered. "Then we'll speak with them here tomorrow afternoon."

"Understood. We'll leave it in your capable hands."

As they wrapped things up, the corners of their mouths had turned up slightly...all because of the two devilish grins they now wore on their faces.

When Kaoru got back to the workshop, she mulled over everything she'd just heard in her head. This time, however, it wasn't to find a way out of this situation. She wanted to hit the enemy with everything she had, and she'd squeeze out every last drop of what she knew to make it happen.

She wasn't going to hold back on using her powers anymore. There were already so many people out there who thought she was some sort of goddess already, and plenty more thought she'd earned the favor of Celes, so nothing would really change from her gaining a few more mysterious powers. It was far more important now to ensure that anyone besides the bad guys and soldiers wouldn't lose their lives in vain.

…That's right, even the soldiers, good or bad. It was their job, after all, and they had chosen that path of their own volition.

She continued thinking things over as she prepared dinner for everyone at the workshop, and even while she cleaned everything up afterward. When she finally decided on her course of action, Kaoru headed off to bed to prepare herself for the next day.

The next day, at the Adan residence, Earl Adan, Roland, Francette, Kaoru, and the group from Rueda were all gathered in the same room. There were guards posted outside the room and around the perimeter of the mansion.

"It's an honor to meet with you, Lady Angel!" Cardinal Whatever-His-Name-Was greeted Kaoru, a smile on his face. He was accompanied by two bishops and several priests, as well.

The cardinal was completely bald and sported a lengthy mustache, and the roundness of his gut told everything one needed to know about the lavish lifestyle he lived. Kaoru had made it clear she didn't want to be called an "angel" or anything of the sort, so either the cardinal hadn't done his research beforehand, or he was doing it on purpose to try and put her on a pedestal.

"No, I'm not Celes's errand girl or anything, and everyone around here knows that. You don't actually know one thing about me, do you?"

The cardinal began sweating a little at Kaoru's chilly response.

"But anyone who delivers the word of Lady Celestine *must* be an angel sent by the Goddess herself!" It seemed the cardinal was fully set on making Kaoru out to be a messenger of the Goddess.

"Hmph, I see… So, why did you ask to see me?"

The cardinal launched into his explanation, doing everything he could to persuade Kaoru after the lukewarm reaction she gave him. "Well, as you may already be aware, the armies of the Aligot Empire are currently on their way here to Grua. That is why we wanted to take you to safety before they arrived. There is no place safer than the Holy Land of Rueda, where we wish to offer you protection at our Grand Temple…"

"But isn't that because Rueda allowed this to happen in the first place?"

"Huh…?" The cardinal found himself at a sudden loss for words.

"Rueda was invaded from the northwest, so why didn't they send word to Balmore? How come you've shown up here in your gaudy carriage, and there haven't been any express horses sent to warn this town about what happened? Considering you must have left immediately after the invasion, don't you think you arrived here a little *too* fast? That the Aligot army invaded this quickly means Rueda didn't even lift a finger to stop it, so why did they let them through without any resistance? And why haven't they tried contacting any other countries to ask them for aid?"

"W-Well… Th-That's…" The cardinal couldn't seem to get an answer out after Kaoru's unexpected verbal lashing.

"…In short, that means Rueda is working with the Aligot forces."

"Ngh…"

Ignoring the now cowed cardinal, Kaoru turned to Roland. "Sir Roland, do you think you could send out a message to the other countries? It should read something like, 'Rueda has betrayed the Goddess Celestine and violated their neutrality by allying with the Aligot Empire.'"

"Wh-What falsehoods! Lies! Deception and slander!" the cardinal shouted, his face turning red.

"Oh? But aren't I supposed to be a holy angel who delivers the word of the Goddess herself?" was Kaoru's cold reply.

"Going against the Holy Land means facing excommunication!" the cardinal frantically screamed back. "Are you saying you're fine with the Kingdom of Balmore being separated from the church of the Goddess?!"

"The only place in danger of that is Rueda," Kaoru said coolly. "The Goddess Celestine said herself that she'd never forgive any corrupt country committing evil deeds in her name. She's fed up with it, so she doesn't want you using her name anymore."

A look of terror crossed the cardinal's face. "Th-That can't be… Rueda is a holy land blessed by the Goddess! It is a country of those who have directly received the Goddess's miracles!"

"No, you've got that part wrong, actually."

"Huh?"

The group from Rueda stared blankly back at Kaoru.

"There just happened to be a distortion there, so Celes took care of it. It's not that the country is blessed or anything; she just took something that had been corrupted and put it back to normal.

It wasn't like she was blessing that particular area more than the

other lands. The ancestors of the people from the temple didn't receive anything, miracles or otherwise. Celes had told them they were getting in the way of her cleaning up the mess there, but they didn't listen. They only stuck around and watched her work from a distance. Celes complained to me about how hard that made it for her to get anything done."

"N-No... That can't be right..."

Kaoru ignored the dumbfounded cardinal and turned to Roland again.

"Sir Roland, do you think you could go ahead and pass a few things along to the other countries? Mainly about what Rueda has been plotting, how they were never a country blessed by anyone in the first place, and are merely the descendants of a group who caused nothing but trouble for the Goddess? Oh, and be sure to let the citizens of Rueda know as well."

"Done and done. I'll send out our fastest messengers on the double."

"W-Wait! Stop it, I beg you! If you do that, then..."

"You did this to yourselves, no?" Kaoru replied, bluntly refusing the cardinal. "Oh, what would you call it when someone invades another country and spreads false information, before trying to drag away someone who's supposed to be a key figure...? Espionage? Sabotage? Either way, I suppose the most appropriate course of action would be to arrest you and have you spill everything you know, wouldn't you agree?"

At Roland's orders, the guards waiting outside the room came in and restrained the envoys from Rueda before hauling them off to the palace.

"I know I'm the one who told you all that, but you really didn't hold back on them, did you…" Roland remarked, impressed.

"Oh no, don't be silly… I'm only just getting started." Kaoru wore a wicked grin on her face.

Why do evil smiles seem to fit her so perfectly… Roland thought to himself.

"Then I'll be counting on you to get the message out to those other countries. I've got a little errand I need to take care of right now."

"Wait, what are you going to do?" Roland had a bad feeling about where this was going…

"I'm thinking of heading out for a bit… I heard there's an army invading that's just ripe for the picking…"

"What?!"

She proclaimed she'd eliminate the entire force coming from Rueda…by herself.

Roland desperately tried to stop her, but Kaoru insisted on going to face them alone. Knowing he was fighting a losing battle against her, Roland reluctantly agreed to a compromise and had her take a few soldiers as escorts. All he could do then was believe in the power of the Goddess. At that point, it might have been a good idea for them to rethink their plans on protecting the capital as well…

"…So, that's why I'll be heading out for a bit. If it comes down to it, take these, and all the money you saved from working, and get far away from here."

Kaoru finished up her simple explanation of what was going on, handing a number of healing potions to the group of seven former street urchins that made up the Eyes of the Goddess. These potions weren't like the mass-produced ones on the market, either, but had effects similar to the tears of the goddess. They also didn't have expiration dates.

As Kaoru went to leave, she suddenly found herself surrounded by the kids.

"We're coming with you."

"No way. There are 20,000 soldiers out there heading straight for us. You could die, you know?"

"We're coming with you!"

Emile, the leader of the group, spoke up.

"If you didn't help us when you did, two or three of us would've been dead by now, with another two or three dead within a couple years. The rest of us would've been killed off in turf wars between other criminals, or captured by the guards for stealing and hanged... But right now, we have a roof over our heads, and a house that doesn't leak when it rains and doesn't let the wind inside. We're all wearing clean clothes and have enough to eat to keep us full. We can actually talk about the future with each other now. We have to repay you for this somehow. And besides..."

"Besides...what?" Kaoru questioned.

"We're the Eyes of the Goddess!" Emile answered, sticking out his chest. "Our job isn't just to go out and gather information for the goddess, but to keep her safe as well!"

The other six children followed his example, puffing out their chests and nodding along. There wasn't even the slightest chance they were going to back down on this.

Chapter 10:
Counterattack

"Huh?"

Roland and Kaoru were in sync as they expressed their disbelief: Roland because he saw the seven children Kaoru had brought with her, and Kaoru because she saw Roland was fully prepared to come along with the soldiers he'd brought.

"It was already bad enough having you go, but why are you bringing kids into this as well?! The youngest one can't be more than seven or eight!"

"Why is someone from the royal family coming with us?!"

Both of them retorted back and forth, attacking one another for their lack of common sense.

Unable to find a way to compromise on the sudden turn of events, they ended up leaving as one. All together, their effective fighting force consisted of Kaoru, the seven children who made up the Eyes of the Goddess, Roland, Francette, eight of the royal guards, and two drivers for the wagons—twenty people total.

Though Kaoru had warned the children they could die out here, she had no intention of putting them in that sort of danger. To prevent that outcome, she had her secret technique: to not give a damn and use everything she had. It wasn't like Celes had given her any restrictions in exchange for all the cheat powers she'd received, though she was hoping she wouldn't have to use them. She'd come up with all sorts of contingency plans, just in case.

Still, there was always a chance for the unexpected to happen. Things would become far worse, in more ways than one, if Roland were to die off. It wasn't exactly ideal to show off her powers in front of people, no matter if they were soldiers, nobles, royals, or otherwise. Human greed knew no bounds, after all.

But it was too late to worry about that now. She was told that the royal guard and wagon drivers had already sworn their undying loyalty and wouldn't reveal any of her secrets, but that didn't matter. The royal family were the ones she didn't want to know her secret the most and, lo and behold, the king's brother was traveling along with their group.

The group from the royal palace was all on horseback, while Kaoru and the kids were traveling by wagon. The wagons weren't anything fancy or extravagant like the nobles would use, but the type of covered wagons you'd find in a caravan. One wagon had Kaoru and the kids, along with some food and water, while the other wagon was packed full of food, water, feed for the horses, and a plethora of camping equipment. The reason Kaoru's wagon had supplies as well was so she could escape with the children if the situation called for it, while the others would stay behind to hold off the enemy for as long as they could.

Even though she'd planned to go on foot and take care of this by herself, that Kaoru suddenly found herself traveling with this hodgepodge of a unit brought a scowl to her face.

It was the day after Kaoru and her group left the capital, and they'd just finished passing through a fairly developed town. From here on out it would be nothing but small villages ahead of them. There was no point in building up any large towns close to a country as small as Rueda, which didn't have any significant industry going for it, so the area ahead of them was dotted with smaller settlements that existed only for the sake of agriculture.

It was around then that Kaoru and the others began preparing for what lay ahead. They instructed the inhabitants of every village they passed through to pack up the bare necessities of their personal belongings, as well as all the food on hand, and evacuate for the time being. The villagers would be able to come back right away, so they directed the people to only take what was important and hide in the mountains. They also went about asking the villagers they met where the wells and other water sources were, taking note of those locations. Judging by when the enemy was expected to arrive and how fast that army was moving, they made sure to stress how important it was to be ready to evacuate at a moment's notice before heading on to the next village.

There wasn't a single person who didn't know of Roland, the king's brother, and if Kaoru (albeit reluctantly) also went so far as to introduce herself as an angel of the Goddess, there wasn't a soul who opposed their idea. By giving potions to those who couldn't move, whether due to injuries or illness, they were able to double the speed at which the villagers could prepare to make an escape.

Six days after leaving the capital—

When Kaoru's group reached a village that was supposed to be around two days away from the encroaching army, they gave the villagers the same instructions to get ready to evacuate. The only difference this time was that they told this village to do so immediately.

Four of the eight royal guards stayed behind to assist and watch over the evacuation. The rest of the group left the wagons and horses behind as well and headed out on foot.

The reason they'd left half of the royal guards behind was because they wouldn't have the luxury of being able to search the village at their leisure afterward. The four guards were insurance in the event the enemy sent out a scout or an advance party to the village before Kaoru and the others could make their way back first.

As they continued on their way the next morning, Francette returned to the group in an outfit that made her look like a simple village girl. She had the most stamina out of all the soldiers traveling with them, so she'd gone out alone to confirm the enemy's location.

"The vanguard of the enemy troops were taking a short rest about two hours ahead of here. At the rate they're moving, I would expect them to arrive in another six hours…"

Judging by it taking two hours for Francette to come back, she could move around four times as fast as it took for the enemy to march.

"It doesn't look like there are any better spots farther ahead, and there's always the chance they could make it here faster than we thought, so let's head back to the gorge we passed by earlier and ambush them there."

With a nod, everyone headed back along the road.

As Kaoru and the others retraced their steps, they'd pushed their way through one of the bumpy, out-of-the-way paths and made it up to a cliff that overlooked the road that ran through the gorge. The kids had trained their legs back when they were thieves…rather, back when they had to work *extra* hard to make a living, so they made it up without much trouble at all.

At the very least, there wasn't anyone among them slower than Kaoru. She'd managed to get through the ordeal by downing potion after potion, but now they were all sloshing around uncomfortably in her stomach.

"They should be here any second now..." Kaoru muttered to herself, turning her attention from the road to look behind her.

There were all sorts of suspicious red and white glass spheres lined up there, all about the size of clenched fists, along with several tree branches around a meter in length, each of which had nets made of vines attached to the end of them. One of the royal guards had come up with the idea after Kaoru created the glass spheres and wondered aloud if there was any way to send them flying farther than when throwing them by hand.

"...They're here."

Francette doesn't just have amazing endurance, she's got eyes like a hawk as well... Dang, just how strong was that potion I gave her?

"It's still not time for us to make our move," Kaoru told the group, "so all I want you to do is stay calm and be careful not to be seen by anyone below us."

The thirteen others silently nodded back in response.

The enemy forces gradually marched closer and closer, eventually advancing right below Kaoru and the others. They were getting ready to carry out their attack on the troops—but it wasn't going to be against the ones at the front.

The Aligot army continued passing by right under their noses.

"Ah..." A slight expression of dull surprise escaped from Roland's lips.

"Something wrong?" Kaoru asked.

"You see that group over there? I'm pretty sure they're the commanders of this army. But I also caught a glimpse of people who looked like priests mixed in with them...and some were armed."

Taking a look for herself, they definitely looked like priests. There were a few who looked like they could even be bishops, while the others wore simple cassocks, and all were outfitted with armor and weapons.

"So not only did Rueda let Aligot pass right through their country and try to hide it, now they're even participating directly... My guess is that they're planning on appealing to the people of the royal capital in the name of the pope and attempting to take the capital's main temple under their control. That, or they were planning on capturing Kaoru in the chaos after they invaded Grua..."

Anger clouded the children's faces after hearing what Roland had said.

It had been some time since the vanguard of the troops had passed them by, and the support troops bringing up the rear were almost directly under the cliff. Everyone in Kaoru's group was in position on top of the cliff, waiting for her signal.

That was when she gave the order:

"Throw the white ones at both ends of the line of support troops!"

The members of Kaoru's group stationed at either end of the cliff began using their homemade slingshots to launch the white orbs at the soldiers below. Booming explosions shook the earth as they made impact after impact with the ground. Pandemonium spread throughout the support troops. The soldiers at the front were desperately looking around for their assailants, but they wouldn't be able to find Kaoru and the others right away, since they'd hidden up on the cliff.

"The red ones next! Fire!"

As the red orbs made contact with the ground, swathes of flame spread out as they shattered on impact. They kept up their bombardment using their slingshots and throwing the glass orbs by hand, fire enveloping the army's wagons one after the other. Unlike the soldiers, it was no easy task for the wagons to move off the road, and they ended up trapped with nowhere to go because of the craters and fires from the explosions cutting off their paths.

The white orbs were packed full of a substance similar to nitroglycerin, their threshold for exploding lowered for the sake of safety. The red orbs, on the other hand, were firebombs brimming with a flammable jelly-like substance made up of napalm and naphtha which was designed to spontaneously ignite once it made contact with the air. Even if you tried dousing the flames in water, they just wouldn't go out.

After focusing their attacks solely on the support troops, Kaoru barked out her next order.

"Launch the red and white orbs toward the back of their main forces!"

Though they knew they were being attacked from the cliff, the archers weren't able to get any shots off at Kaoru and the others because they would immediately back away after throwing a glass orb. The soldiers couldn't exactly scramble up the cliffside to get to them right away, either. The only thing the army could do was take the full brunt of the one-sided attack.

Kaoru had begun the attack by focusing only on the support troops, but slowly changed targets to the main body of soldiers in the center, causing them to fly into a panic. They raced forward in a desperate attempt to escape the blast zone, yelling at the soldiers in front of them all the while. The soldiers ahead realized what was going on and began sprinting for dear life, but couldn't move fast enough due to the heavy armor they wore. Despite this setback, they were all frantic to escape the hellish gorge as fast as humanly possible.

It was only after the Aligot army had made it out of the gorge and cautiously caught their breath when they finally realized something: The support troops weren't following them.

When the soldiers went back to check on them, the surviving support troops were standing in a daze beside the wreckage of their wagons. Said wagons had carried their food, water, feed for horses, arrows, spare equipment, camping goods, weapons, and all sorts of other supplies…and they'd lost almost all of it in the attack.

Around that same time, Kaoru's group had used the mountain trail to get in front of the Aligot army, emerging back onto the main road and heading toward the village.

Despite having women and children with them, they still moved much faster than the heavily armored soldiers. Besides the energy the Aligot troops spent fleeing from the attack, the soldiers most likely had their hands full dealing with the loss of their support troops and trying to come up with countermeasures to cope with it as well. It was almost guaranteed they wouldn't try moving anywhere else today. That's why Kaoru determined they should have a whole day's head start on the troops.

All that was left was for her to prepare their invitation to hell…

The villagers had already finished evacuating by the time Kaoru and the others returned, and they were greeted by the four royal guards they'd left on standby. Luckily for them, they didn't have any run-ins with enemy scouts or advance parties.

"All right, I want everyone to get ready to move out. First, fill up on all the water you can. After I'm done with the well, you are *absolutely not* allowed to take any more water from it."

Finished with her warning, Kaoru went house-to-house to check if the villagers had left any food or water behind. She either threw away the leftover water she found in bottles or pots, or instead poured a suspicious liquid into it. There was barely any food that hadn't already been taken away, but she sprinkled this liquid over the little she managed to scrounge up as well.

When she finished checking all the houses, Kaoru headed out to the fields and began shoving all sorts of things into her Item Box.

After confirming that everyone had stocked up on water, she pulled out the notes she had taken the other day and visited each of the wells in the village, pouring more of the sketchy liquid into every one of them.

"All right, let's get going!"

They retraced their steps and went back to the next village, now completely devoid of people since the evacuations had finished.

The wagons they initially came with had become lighter after using up some of their supplies, meaning that they could move at a pace faster than the Aligot army could ever hope to keep up with. They wouldn't have to worry about the soldiers catching up to them, even if Kaoru took extra time to do some…"preparations" of her own.

They also took the chance to send one of the royal guards back to the capital as a messenger, asking them to relay a single message:

"Everything is going according to plan."

"All our supplies have been destroyed?!" the general of Aligot's northern invasion forces said, taken aback when he heard the news.

"Affirmative. We've gathered up what wasn't burnt during the attack, but we've lost almost all our reserve weapons and outdoor camping gear. We only have enough water to last two days, and only about a day's worth of food…"

"Even the siege weapons?!"

"Yes, sir…"

Their mission was to lay siege to Grua and storm the castle, and it had to be done before Balmore's main forces returned. But even if the majority of the enemy's troops were being distracted by the empire's forces to the west, they'd have a hell of a time fighting against an enemy holed up behind their walls without proper siege equipment.

Most importantly, there wasn't anyone stupid enough to wage a battle of endurance against an enemy they were supposed to be laying siege to. They'd estimated the capital would have less than 10,000 troops available, but that wouldn't mean a thing if the besiegers didn't have the supplies to support their own troops.

However...

"How many settlements are ahead of us?"

"Six villages and one medium-sized town between our current position and the capital, sir."

"Good. Send a messenger to Rueda with a request for food, water, and other necessary supplies. We'll continue pressing ahead and commandeer what we can from the settlements we come across— emergency food stores, crops, livestock...everything. We won't leave even a single seed for next year's crops behind! There will be no food distribution until we reach the next town, and water rations will only be a third of the usual amount. The troops should be able to endure that for a day."

Retreat had never been an option for them. The fate of the empire was riding on this invasion, and their comrades to the west were risking their lives acting as a distraction for the brunt of Balmore's forces. They couldn't return home with the paltry excuse of running out of food and water. The commanding officers would all surely hang.

The northern Aligot forces resumed their march on Grua, the capital of the Kingdom of Balmore.

"What was that?!"

After enduring empty stomachs and crippling thirst, the empire's troops had finally managed to make it to the village. The general had arrived at the village a bit later than the vanguard of their forces when he received an alarming report: all of the soldiers who'd taken water from the wells were now violently throwing up and suffering from severe diarrhea. Those who had happened to sample the food and water they'd found in the houses were suffering the same fate.

"Damn them... Those Balmore bastards poisoned the wells! Where are the villagers?!"

"There's not a single one to be found, sir."

"So they were evacuated... Search for any hidden food stores, and any crops as well!"

The soldiers spread out in all directions after receiving their orders.

The enemy had to be out of their minds to actually dump poison into the wells. Even if it successfully drove the army away, they'd have to draw out all the water in the well, just to purify the water. At worst, it could even spread to the main water source and end up contaminating the other wells. It was something that no sane villager would agree to.

A short while later, the soldiers returned to make their reports. There wasn't any food to be found, and not even the slightest hint of any crops left in the fields.

"Staying here without food or water will only exhaust the troops further. Get them ready to head out again, double time! We're heading to the next village!"

In the back of his mind, the general couldn't shake the thought that the next village would end up being barren as well. Depending on how long it took for the messenger they had sent to reach Rueda, the time it would take for them to prepare the supplies and the wagons, and the days it would take to get them here, who knew how long it would be until they saw food and water again? And that was only if Rueda was willing to take on something that wasn't part of their initial secret agreement.

Though food and weapons were important, the biggest problem they were dealing with was water. There weren't that many rivers in this part of the country, and they wouldn't be running into any others on their way to Grua. The farms here were smaller, since the crops raised depended on rain and the water drawn from the wells to grow, with only a couple dozen settlements sparsely dotted along the path they'd be taking. If all the wells had been poisoned, they wouldn't have any hope of refilling their water supplies. But if they could just reach the town right before the capital...

Unlike these small villages, it'd be impossible for them to evacuate every single person living there. There could be people intentionally defying the order to evacuate, or some who didn't have any other place to stay. There may have been others who were too old or had injuries that kept them from moving anywhere else. Emptying the entire town of all food would be an impossible task, and they wouldn't be able to chuck poison into the wells if they wanted it to stay inhabitable later on.

The capital's forces were all holed up in the city, so their main goal would be to occupy the town and commandeer its supplies, along with what they could get from the surrounding villages. That should let their soldiers recuperate somewhat while they waited for Rueda to send aid. They'd wait a while after taking the town, and if the supplies still hadn't arrived, they'd lay siege to the capital, regardless. They could just keep taking what supplies they needed from the area around them, and it was a simple task to fashion together some siege equipment on the spot. It wasn't the hardest thing in the world to make grappling hooks or a simple battering ram, after all.

Unlike the troops in the capital, they had the villages and towns to rely on, and with everything the citizens in Balmore had to take care of, they'd be burning through supplies much faster, as well. Even if Balmore's main forces did return, the empire's forces to the west could follow them and execute a pincer attack. The general in charge of the northern forces knew it was just wishful thinking on his part...but he was going to bet on that chance. He didn't have any other choice.

They'd sent soldiers ahead on horseback in the hopes that they could prevent more wells from being poisoned. But when they arrived in the next town, the wells had been contaminated all the same. There wasn't a scrap of food to be found, and rations were cut to a quarter of what they had been, as they headed for the next town.

Kaoru and the others had finished sabotaging the fourth town, and would be arriving at the fifth before long.

"I wonder if it's working..." Kaoru muttered to herself.

"I'm sure they must be trying to deal with the lack of water right about now," Roland answered. "They're soldiers forced to march out there under the blazing hot sun. If they don't get enough water, the fatigue and internal damage should be enough to start dropping them like flies. Some of them will even drink the water from the wells, knowing it'll wreck their stomachs."

"Yeah..."

Even if they knew what it would do to them, they wouldn't be able to bear the thirst and would end up drinking it anyway. That's why Kaoru had decided to go with something that caused vomiting and diarrhea instead of straight-up death. They'd be able to slake their thirst if they drank the contaminated water, but they'd end up losing more liquid than they were getting from it, causing them to be worse off than before.

They wouldn't be in any condition to keep marching with their heavy armor, so their only options were to leave it behind, or to have others help them. Either way, it would end up slowing them down. To an army, being burdened with the infirm and wounded was worse than having their people killed in battle.

Right as they were getting close to the next village, Kaoru and the others found a little boy walking along the road toward them. Kaoru had a bad feeling about this, and she stopped the wagon so she could talk with him.

"What's wrong? You didn't evacuate with everyone else?" Kaoru questioned as she stepped down from the wagon.

"We're in trouble, Miss Angel! The bad guys found a well!"

Shocked, Kaoru pressed him for more information. Apparently, there was a hidden well located in the village they'd left earlier that morning. For some reason, this one almost never dried up, even during the harshest of droughts. It was kept hidden from the other villages so they wouldn't try to rush it during one of the dry spells that happened every few decades—and the villagers also hadn't told Kaoru and the others about it. It could've been because they wanted the well to stay hidden, or they were afraid that something might happen to it if they spilled the beans, or even because they thought the empire wouldn't be able to find it so easily.

But the boy had overheard what three of the other villagers had been whispering to each other. They'd double back and return to the village, selling the information about the hidden well to the empire and getting rich from it. After the soldiers left, they'd raid all the villagers' homes and steal as many valuables as they could throw onto a cart before heading straight to Rueda.

After the three men had disappeared, the boy had run to the adults to let them know what he heard. The men in question were burly with violent dispositions, however, and the villagers didn't exactly want to catch up with them and risk getting killed in the process. That was why they decided to ignore them and head straight to the capital.

After spending a night in the neighboring village, the boy had told his family he was going to take a walk with his friends before secretly sneaking away from the group and heading back to warn Kaoru and the others.

"Why didn't you leave with everyone else? It's dangerous here," Kaoru asked the boy.

"Ginnie was saved because of the medicine we got from the Goddess."

Kaoru didn't know if Ginnie was part of this kid's family or just a friend, or whatever, but she'd seen the look he was giving her more times than she could count. He wouldn't listen even if she explained, and she didn't have time for it either.

"Can I ask you to guide us there?"

"Of course!"

Kaoru left two royal guards behind to watch over the other two wells with some spare bottles of poison. She took the rest with her back to the other village. They should still have a good two days' head start on the empire's troops, so they'd be able to make the return trip without the empire's army catching up to them. They'd already finished sabotaging that village, so if they could just poison that last hidden well, then that would be it.

But just like the enemy general, that was nothing more than wishful thinking on their part...

Chapter 11:
Hell

With Tapani leading the way, Kaoru and the others headed to a small house on the outskirts of the village they'd left earlier. A small building had been constructed around the hidden well, so it didn't look like anything more than a storage shed from the outside.

"It's that cabin over there," Tapani said, pointing.

As Kaoru and the others stepped down from the wagon to get closer, a group of twenty soldiers on horseback headed toward them from the center of the village.

"Damn it, they sent troops ahead!" Roland cursed under his breath, drawing his sword. Francette and the five royal guards followed suit.

Though they were outnumbered three-to-one, they had Roland, a man famed for his bravery, and a group of elite knights with them. That Francette only looked like a knight-in-training would cause most people to underestimate her true abilities, which were vastly superior compared to what they were before she drank the potion Kaoru had given her (she had still been incredibly talented before drinking it, though).

On the other hand, the Aligot troops were dehydrated, underfed, and exhausted. Even the horses they were riding on looked exhausted. Thinking they should be able to handle anything that came their way, Kaoru headed toward the shed. Tapani and the other eight children followed after her.

Four of the children stood in front of the shed to guard the entrance. They appeared to be empty-handed, but each one of them carried a knife hidden in one of their pockets. It was a strategy that would turn them being children kids into an asset; hopefully they could catch the soldiers off guard and start slashing if the situation called for it.

Kaoru took a single bottle from her Item Box and gripped it tightly in her left hand. It was a pain in the butt to decide what the potion would do every time she made them, so she had decided to make them and stuff them into her Item Box in advance.

When she opened the door and walked inside the dim shed with the other kids...they were met face-to-face with three Aligot soldiers. It seemed like the soldiers hadn't just arrived after all.

"Who are you supposed to be?" one of the soldiers said after scooping up some water to drink.

The five of them froze up on the spot. There was no way they could tell them the truth. Suddenly, one of the soldiers noticed the bottle Kaoru was holding in her hand.

"Hey! What's that?! Answer me!"

By the time Kaoru realized her mistake, it was already too late.

"Wait a second... Were *you* the ones poisoning the wells?"

The soldiers set down their wooden cups and stood up.

Kaoru hesitated, unsure of what to do next. An explosion would attract attention from the soldiers outside. No matter how strong Roland and the others were, they were still outnumbered, and it could end up being a real struggle for them to fend off any more reinforcements that came to the shed.

But how could she incapacitate them? Hydrochloric acid? Maybe sulfuric acid? If they started screaming, reinforcements would still come running. It wasn't that hard to take down soldiers if she really put her mind to it, and it wasn't like they would cut down a bunch of kids out of nowhere, either.

Kaoru had taken advantage of the lull to wrack her brain for a plan. The kids took that as a sign that she was out of options and didn't know what to do.

"…Huh?"

The youngest child of the group, the eight-year-old Belle, had snatched the bottle from Kaoru's hand and began trotting over to the soldiers. Kaoru reached out to try and stop her, but Emile held her back.

"It's alright. Belle will take care of it."

Kaoru didn't know what Emile was trying to say.

The soldiers grinned as they watched Belle toddle toward them, bottle pressed against her chest. It was going to be a piece of cake to catch a little girl like her—or, to be more accurate, child's play. She was heading straight toward them, and she would have to move her arms if she was going to get ready to pop off the lid to the bottle or throw it into the well. Either way, they'd stop her or make her slow down before that happened.

She was still walking straight ahead. If she tried throwing it now, the three would just smack it away. The soldiers stood in front of the well, blocking her.

Suddenly, Belle stepped hard off her left foot and dodged to the right, breaking into a full-on sprint, and dodged between them. They each only had one arm available to try and stop her now, as soldier thought that the one next to him would do so. With their guards completely down, she aimed for the easiest spot to run between them.

It was a technique she'd perfected during her time as a street urchin, and was necessary to survive when trying to escape while surrounded by adults. She folded her arms and ducked down low,

73

not losing any of her speed even as she minimized her chance of being captured and opened the lid of the bottle. The slow, tottering jog from earlier had been a feint, since she was actually the fastest sprinter of all the children. After she managed to slip through the soldiers, she dove headfirst...right into the well.

"What...?" Kaoru was shocked speechless.

"I told you, didn't I? Belle took care of it," Emile responded.

Kaoru couldn't believe the words coming out of his mouth. His face was completely expressionless.

"But why?! Why would she do something as stupid as that?!" Kaoru shouted furiously.

"If you hadn't given her that medicine, Belle would already be dead," Emile answered calmly. "The happy days she got to live because of that were more than worth paying for with her life. And... And Belle was one of the Eyes of the Goddess."

"Don't gimme that crap!"

Kaoru was inches away from socking Emile off his feet...but when she caught a look at his face, she could see the tears running down his cheeks. Kaoru slowly lowered her arm.

"You idiot..."

It was then the dazed soldiers finally came back to their senses...

"Y-You damn brats... What have you done?!"

"That was the only safe well we had... It was our only hope..."

The soldiers drew their swords, seething with anger over losing any hope they had for the future because they underestimated a child. Kaoru could see it in their eyes: they were going to kill the children.

But it wasn't just the soldiers who were blind with rage.

"...Die."

At Kaoru's words, the soldiers began writhing in agony. One lost the ability to breathe, drowning on dry land as his lungs suddenly filled with water. Another clutched at his midsection, his insides slowly melting away from having his stomach acid suddenly released throughout his body. The last one was robbed of his ability to move because of the poison spreading throughout his body, his breathing slowly becoming more shallow as his heartbeat became weaker.

The soldiers finally succumbed.

"This is only the beginning," Kaoru muttered.

There was no way for the kids to know the meaning behind those ominous words.

Before Kaoru knew it, Emile had sprinted to the well and was just about to throw himself down.

"What are you doing?"

"Belle might still be alive. I have to save her!"

"No need," Kaoru responded.

"What are you saying..." Emile asked back, dumbstruck.

Kaoru stuck out her left hand, and in the next instant, a little girl stood where she was pointing.

"H-Huh? But I was..."

"Belle!!!"

Back when Kaoru was negotiating with Celes for her Item Box, the goddess was kind enough not to place any restrictions on how she could use it. Not only was time frozen inside it, but since it was connected to a different dimension, there were no problems storing living things inside. And since it existed inside that different dimension, there was no need to physically touch what she wanted to put inside, either.

Kaoru had stored Belle in her Item Box as soon as she dove into the well. She'd gone in headfirst, after all, so there was a chance she could have ended up hurt, or worse—dead.

It was a mystery why no one had thought it strange that there was no splash after she jumped.

"Emile, I want you to give everyone a message from me: If you've all offered your lives to me, then you don't get to die without my permission. Got it?"

Emile nodded over and over again, tears streaming down his face as he held Belle close. Tapani could only watch on, his mouth agape, after bearing witness to a bona fide miracle.

Kaoru had stored the bottle of poison inside her Item Box along with Belle, so they still had to toss that into the well. By the time they'd all left the shack, the battle outside was just wrapping up.

The remaining enemy soldiers were busy fleeing for dear life. Since there wasn't anything they needed to hide anymore, there was no reason to finish them all off. In fact, having the escaping soldiers tell their comrades that there weren't any more safe wells could completely crush their already low morale.

Kaoru's group had taken some casualties, as well. One of the royal guards had a shallow cut on their arm, while two others bore deep gashes. Luckily for them, none of the enemy knights on horseback were able to land any killing blows after being knocked off their mounts. This meant that Roland and the others could focus on other targets once they were incapacitated.

Kaoru made sure all of them had made a complete recovery after creating a few more potions. The other royal guards were shocked after seeing their first miracle with their own eyes. While they may have seen what the potions on the market were able to do, the potions Kaoru had just used were on a completely different level.

Some of the Aligot troops had met their end in the fight earlier, but there were still plenty of survivors. Roland was going back and forth on whether to finish them off, since he didn't want any extra baggage to carry, but eventually decided on tying them up and healing them just enough so that they weren't on the brink of death. They'd made some space in their wagon after using up some of their supplies, so now they had enough room for the ten prisoners of war they found themselves with.

After taking a quick look around the village, they happened upon three corpses. According to Tapani, those were the same villagers who had been trying to sell out to the empire. There was no reason for the Aligot troops to pay them a single coin once they knew where the well was, and they *were* an invading army, after all, so it was a fitting end for a trio that had been so shallow-minded. It looked like they'd met their maker before stealing any of the villagers' possessions, too, so everything worked out in the end.

All of the Aligot advance party had ridden in on horseback, so Kaoru's group went ahead and took possession of the horses they used. None of the horses had been killed in the battle, luckily enough, so Kaoru was able to patch all of them up with potions.

The horses had all but recognized Kaoru as their new owner. Horses fetched a high price at market, and that went doubly so for war-trained horses. To Kaoru, these horses were so, *so* much more valuable than the prisoners they'd captured.

Horses and prisoners in tow, Kaoru and the others went on their way back to the fifth village. Along the way, they met up with the other two royal guards they'd left behind to finish poisoning the wells. They'd finished what needed to be done, and had been on their way to regroup with everyone.

After double-checking to make sure everything had been properly sabotaged, the group made their way back to the royal capital.

It had been six days since the Aligot forces to the north had suffered heavy losses to their supplies. All six of the villages they'd passed along the way had been contaminated by poison, and there wasn't even a crumb of food to be found anywhere. They were overjoyed to hear that the scouting party they'd sent ahead to the fourth village had located an untainted well, but those hopes were quickly dashed when they clashed with Balmore's forces and were almost completely wiped out. The soldiers hoped that the group didn't have anything to do with whoever was poisoning the water supplies, or that they didn't know about the well since it was hidden... But by the time they reached the village, the well was already contaminated.

Judging by the corpses around the well, it looked like this group had known about the well from the beginning. They must have realized they'd missed a well and had come back to take care of it. Normally, it would be a complete disgrace that twenty of the mighty Aligot Empire's soldiers had been defeated by a mere seven soldiers, but one of the people who survived the encounter said he heard one of the group from Balmore use the name "Roland."

If that was true, then they could take that to mean "Fearsome Fran" was with him as well, a mysterious and frighteningly powerful girl who'd been assigned as Roland's personal guard. If that were the case, it was easy to see how the battle turned out the way it did. That said, it was also easy to tell what fate awaited those who ran away once they returned to Aligot, *if* they managed to make it back home at all.

At the very least, they'd keep putting their soldiers to work as they continued their invasion. There was no need to hinder their troops' fighting potential any more than they already had. They'd already run out of food, and their water supplies would run dry today, as well. They'd dismounted from their horses to try and reduce the amount of stress put on them, but the horses were still collapsing all the same.

Tears in their eyes, the riders cut the horses' arteries and offered the blood and meat to the famished and dehydrated soldiers. For them, it was the same thing as cutting up and eating their human comrades. The only thing they could do was fight back the urge to cry, because every tear they shed meant wasting the precious fluids they'd worked so hard to drink.

Just eating meat took fluids as well, which only made their thirst that much worse. The saliva that came from it was nothing more than temporary relief, since they barely had enough water in their bodies for that in the first place.

They left those who'd drunk the tainted water on the side of the road. They'd tried bringing them along at first, but the afflicted soldiers needed substantial amounts of water to survive after expelling so much liquid. There wasn't much they could do for those who drank the water at the first village without knowing it was tainted, but the guilt they felt over leaving the ones they had tried the water elsewhere was tearing them apart.

There were many soldiers who snuck off to drink the water from the wells, unable to bear it any longer. Their thirst was slaked in a moment of pure bliss...until about thirty minutes later, which was when the symptoms kicked in.

Finally, the ones who hadn't drunk the water began collapsing from dehydration and heatstroke. They'd have been fine if they had rested in a cool spot and were given some salt and water to drink— but that was the problem. They didn't have the supplies to recover, they didn't have any place to rest, and they didn't have any wagons to be put on, either. They could only lay by the side of the road, the wails of dying men surrounding them from all sides as the soldiers marched on.

Take me with you...

Don't leave me here...

I don't want to die here...

I want to go home alive...

My newborn daughter is waiting for me...

The soldiers kept their eyes pointing strictly ahead, grimacing as they did everything they could to avoid meeting the gazes of those around them. They couldn't look at them; they couldn't listen to them; most of all, they couldn't cry for them. The lives of their comrades' horses would all be for naught.

It was a living hell. They could have at least died with honor if they'd fallen in battle. But instead, here they were, dying on the side of the road in another country while covered in their own waste.

It was too horrible to bear. Would they have to trek back through here, as well? Would they have to listen to the same pitiful cries, then, too? Would they even survive until then?

The clergymen from Rueda didn't look any better. Would they be able to preach the mercy of the Goddess to those laid out on either side of the road? Right now, it seemed like it'd be easier for them to explain if it had been the work of the devil.

The person who brought them here was none other than the devil—and this was hell.

Only one day left. They'd arrive in town by tomorrow.

They could fill up on all the food and water they could ever want, and the soldiers would finally have a chance to rest. They'd no longer be a group of shambling soldiers with broken spirits, and the mighty army of the Aligot Empire would come back to life once more. All they had to do was march on the defenseless town and make it their own.

The next day…

The Aligot forces had finally arrived at the outskirts of Nicosia, a town that was only a day away from the capital of Balmore.

After rounding the last hill, the soldiers leading the troops should have been able to see the town, but for some reason, they suddenly came to a halt. The formation of the troops behind them began falling apart since they were now blocking the way forward.

The officers were furious over the vanguard's apparent ineptitude in keeping them from the one place that was giving their troops hope, and sent out a horse to the front of the army. They'd given it plenty of water, so they could use it for sending messages.

When the commanding officer finally made it to the front troops, he froze just like everyone else.

Standing between them and Nicosia were 12,000 Balmore troops. Besides the 3,000 they'd left to guard the castle, it was the full brunt of the forces assigned to protect the capital.

"No… It can't be…" the commander lamented, crumpling down on the spot.

"They weren't all stationed inside the capital?" The same expression of despair clouded the general's face when he reached the front lines.

"Even with more than half our army with us, our troops had to walk all the way here, while Balmore's soldiers are in peak condition. They've even set up simple encampments outside the town. This won't even be a fight…"

In war, it wasn't as if every single soldier on each side fought all at once. If that was how it worked, 10,000 soldiers on each side would all be going up against each other at once. Even with how weak they were, the Aligot troops would still have had a chance at winning the battle.

In reality, it was only the vanguard of each side's armies fighting, while the soldiers behind them replaced the fallen as the battle raged on. The number of soldiers actually fighting on each side would always stay roughly the same. That way, the weaker side would just keep on losing as the fighting continued.

There was no hope of victory for them now. Even if they wanted to retreat, their soldiers didn't have the strength to keep marching. All that awaited them on the way back were wells full of contaminated water, and at the rate they'd be staggering along, the enemy could catch up to them in no time and launch an assault from behind.

The only thing that would happen from recklessly charging into a fight was 20,000 of the Aligot Empire's precious soldiers dying in vain. If that were the case, knowing when to give up and choose the option that might let them go home after the war finished was the obvious choice here. It wasn't like the empire's defeat was certain, either.

The general would take all the responsibility that came with surrendering. It was a small price to pay in exchange for 20,000 of their soldiers' lives.

There was little chance that Balmore was just going to execute every last one of them, and it'd definitely be a burden to try and feed 20,000 prisoners of war. No matter which side was victorious, it wouldn't be long until the soldiers could see their homes once more.

"We're surrendering. Prepare to send out a messenger immediately!"

The regret was obvious in the faces of the troops, but no one tried opposing him.

"Get on it, now! We may still be able to save the people we left behind, so we don't have time to waste!"

Finally realizing the implications behind his command, the officers all scrambled to get it done.

"Is it over?"

"Looks like it..." came Roland's response, standing together with Kaoru, both of them a fair distance behind the troops that had been deployed to Nicosia.

It looked like the villagers would be able to get back home sooner than they first thought. The poison in the wells would lose their effectiveness after ten days had passed, since Kaoru didn't want to make the wells completely unusable in the event that something happened to her.

Even if they didn't wait out the ten days, they could purify the wells right away if they threw in one of the potions Kaoru had given them. She'd still have to make sure to continue reminding them not to eat or drink any of the other food and water in their homes until after the ten days had passed or they had used one of the antidotes. But even then, they'd be fine as long as they got plenty of water—though they'd still have to put up with suffering with severe diarrhea for a few days.

"This was all so underhanded..."

"Would you rather we confronted them head-on in a fair fight, and had thousands die because of it?"

"N-No, I didn't mean it like that..."

Having put so much effort into becoming the ideal knight, Francette was having trouble accepting the methods they'd used.

But she could never say she wanted other soldiers to die just so she could be satisfied.

"I want you all to go back to the capital," Kaoru said as she turned to the eight children, Tapani included. He'd made himself right at home with the other orphans, but why he hadn't gone back to his parents yet was a mystery to her.

"Are you saying you're not coming with us?" Emile fired back.

"That's right. I can't have you coming with me this time."

"But why?! We can still be a shield for you!"

"That's exactly why I'm telling you no! Someone could have their head sliced off next time, or get stabbed through the heart. I wouldn't know what to do with myself if that happened. If I'm on my own, though, I should be able to handle anything that comes my way."

That was all a big fat lie, though. Even Kaoru wouldn't be able to do anything with potions if she was decapitated or stabbed through the heart. Regardless, she had no intention of getting herself in a situation like that in the first place.

"So, does that mean you think we'd just get in your way?"

Kaoru hesitated a moment before giving it to them straight. "… You are. You're all still too weak."

Emile fell silent as he hung his head.

"But don't get the wrong idea. You're only weak for the time being. You're still kids, so there's no helping that. And I'm not saying you have to get as strong as Francette, either."

Francette was taken by surprise over suddenly being used as an example like that.

"I'm also not saying that you're completely useless. While I'm out there doing what I'm best at, I want you to help me out by doing the sort of work *you're* all best at."

The seven members of the Eyes of the Goddess (plus one) reluctantly gave in to her reasoning.

...I guess I can just say there's eight of them now. He pretty much fits right in.

With that, the children all clambered onto a wagon and headed back to the royal capital. They'd go and keep an eye on the other nobles and people in power to see what they were saying, taking the opportunity to scour out those with connections to other countries who seemed most likely to be plotting something.

It'd be great if they did dig up any conspiracies or the like, but actually catching wind of any of those would be pretty hard. If it was enough to get the kids on their way back to the capital, though, then that was more than good enough for her.

"...So, what are you planning on doing this time?" Roland asked Kaoru after the wagon carrying the kids had departed.

"Me? I think I'll head over to the battlefield in the west."

"There's no way I'd let you do that!" Roland roared.

But Kaoru wasn't having it.

"I don't need your permission, Sir Roland. I'm just a girl from another country who wandered into the capital. Now, I'll be wandering over to the west, is all."

"Wh—What are you..." Roland's face had turned an entirely different shade of white by this point.

Suddenly, he regained his composure, and a grin stretched across his face.

"So, how exactly are you planning on heading west? There aren't any merchants traveling in that direction right now, nor are there any wagons you can charter. The only way to get there would be for you to walk on your own two feet. How many days do you think that will take? I'm not letting you borrow any carriages or riders from the royal palace, of course."

Roland wore a triumphant look on his face, confident that it was enough to reach a stalemate, since Kaoru shouldn't know how to ride a horse.

"Oh? Then I guess I'll go see if I can't pull some strings."

"Huh?"

Roland stared back at Kaoru blankly as she casually strolled toward the horses they'd "acquired" from the Aligot forces back from the skirmish in the village.

"Hey there, would anyone mind letting me ride them on a little journey to the west together?"

The eighteen horses were all taken aback.

"A-Are you some sort of new horse, missy?" a chestnut-colored horse asked back in shock.

"Nope, I'm just a human who happens to know the goddess of this world, that's all."

"Like hell that makes you a normal human!!!"

Who would've thought I'd get backtalk from horses?

"Anyway, putting that aside for now… I'll completely heal any wounds or diseases for whoever comes with me on the trip, and I'll get you tons of delicious food as well. When the journey's all said and done, I'll buy whatever mare you had your eye on and leave her with you."

"Are you foaling us?!"

"Me! Me!" "No, take me!" *"Can it, whippersnapper! Respect your elders and let me do it, dammit!"*

All hell had broken loose among the horses...

"U-Um, Kaoru? They're all whinnying something fierce... What's going on?"

"Oh, that? They're fighting over who gets to let me ride on them."

"Are you *kidding* me?!"

Chapter 12:
Journey to the West

After deciding which horse to take with me, I set off westward right away. I thought something like this might happen, which was exactly why I had the Item Box. I'd packed all sorts of supplies in case I needed to make an impromptu escape, including food, water, tents, blankets, cookware, weapons, armor, fodder, water buckets—you name it.

Roland, Francette, and four of the royal guards had frantically chased after me, though.

I wonder what they're planning to do about food and stuff... Maybe that's why they left the other three guards behind?

After going through and interviewing all the horses, I'd decided on a six-year-old stallion with a white coat. He had black eyes, and was probably between twenty-two and twenty-nine years old in human years. I wasn't too sure about the conversion between horse and human years though. I wanted to avoid horses that were too young to have much experience or those too old and weak to take on the journey, which was why I decided on him.

He was deeply loyal to me since I'd saved him from a near-fatal sword wound back at the battle in the village. He was cheerful and energetic as well, so bonus points for all that. Having a white mane would make it easier to be spotted by the enemy, but that worked out fine since I had a feeling I'd end up needing to stand out this time.

There were mares among the eighteen horses from before that I would've offered to buy any stallion they had their eye on, but it just so happened that a stallion fit exactly what I was looking for.

I had Francette take care of setting up the reigns and the saddle, since I didn't want to fall off the horse along the way. I never had any experience handling horses or riding gear. The saddle was there so I wouldn't be taking any spills or sliding off the horse or anything. I'd be giving him instructions on how to move myself, so we were fine there.

I didn't have the kids or any sort of luggage to worry about, so as long as I ignored the fact that Roland and the others were following me, all I had to do was ride as fast as I could. That's why the most important issue here was making it so a beginner like me wouldn't fall off during the journey.

It's not like I needed to be able to move however I wanted, so I would've been fine without a saddle or anything. The only problem with that, though, was I could only imagine how rough that would be on my poor body, and I'm kinda afraid what other people would think about me doing that. That's why I ended up going with the more traditional approach to horseback riding.

Instead of heading south from Nicosia toward the capital, I took a separate route to the southwest that led to the main road that stretched out to the west of Grua. Following right behind me was the group from the royal palace who were determined to protect me.

The group following behind me and Ed, the horse I was riding, was having a bit of trouble keeping up as we galloped along at full speed. That's why I imagined they were pretty grateful for the multiple breaks I had to take with how sore my butt and hips were getting.

Even though I was a complete beginner to riding, my horse and I were completely in sync. They'd never be able to follow me if they loaded their horses with all their gear or had a wagon packed full of all the supplies they needed. There weren't really any major problems with me spending the night in a town or village or something, but camping outside would drain Roland's supplies like crazy. Would they go around restocking as they followed me?

While I can't say I wasn't worried about that, I was flying completely solo this time, and Roland had already made clear he wasn't happy about it. Even if they were following close behind me, I didn't have any sort of obligation to split my stockpile with them. I'd be fine with it if they were friends or helping me out, but I'm the type of person who gives the cold shoulder to people who try to get in my way.

I don't have to do jack squat *for them!*

...The group in question Kaoru had directed those thoughts toward didn't know about Kaoru's Item Box, so they hadn't expected her to camp out in the wilderness. She didn't have any sort of luggage with her whatsoever, so they'd been sure she was going to spend the night at an inn, or at worst, ask to stay in someone's house.

There were only a few hours left before the despair began settling in among the group.

"It appears Miss Kaoru isn't planning on stopping in town, Sir Roland... There won't be any other villages or towns for quite some time either," one of the royal guards said as he reported to Roland.

"Hmm... Maybe she just isn't familiar with the terrain to know that?"

"No," Francette cut in, "Kaoru definitely has a map of the area, and it certainly seemed like she knew how to read it."

There was only around an hour left before it would get dark. That was only going to make it harder on everyone, but there was no way around it.

They had to keep following after Kaoru.

"How about we get ready to call it a day, Ed?"

"*You got it, little missy,*" Ed replied, slowing down to a more relaxed gait.

"That spot over there. Let's go a little deeper into those trees so no one can see us from the road. Then we'll make ourselves a place to turn in for the night."

Ed and Kaoru headed off the main road, pushing through the dense clumps of trees.

"S-Sir Roland…"

"Yes, it looks like they're making camp."

"Wh-What shall we do?"

"Not much to say to that, I'm afraid…"

In the end, four of the royal guards headed back to the town they'd passed to acquire the necessities to keep them all going. Horses need plenty of water to work, and while they'd made sure theirs drank plenty back in town, it still put great stress on the horses to carry all their supplies to their campsite. They were lucky enough to have a town close by this time, but things could get hairy if they were out roughing it in the wild with no settlements around.

More than that, Kaoru had no supplies with her, so how was she even getting by in the first place? That was the question on Roland's mind, but there was no way he could just go over and sneak a peek at her while she was sleeping or anything. All he could do was wait and brood over it by himself.

Around that same time, Kaoru and Ed were enjoying dinner together. Kaoru had stocked up on plenty of hot food she'd made in the kitchen back at the workshop. After Ed had finished the feed Kaoru gave him, he was absolutely over the moon as she pulled out one treat after another from her Item Box: corn, carrots, apples, and even sugar cubes. She'd made the sugar cubes with her potion-making abilities, specifying it as a sort of medicine to replenish one's sugar intake that looked, tasted, and was made with the same ingredients as a regular sugar cube.

"This is amazin', it's just like you said! I'm gonna give it all I got again tomorrow, too!"

"Please and thank you. Oh, and drink this, too. It will greatly refresh you."

"Well, thank you kindly."

After sprinkling monster- and bug-repellant potion everywhere, Kaoru pulled out the bed she'd nabbed from the baron's mansion and had herself a good night's rest.

It was the first time in forever she'd pulled out that bed...

The next morning, Kaoru and Ed woke up feeling refreshed and rejuvenated. After enjoying a bit of breakfast and taking care of their business, they set off, as happy as could be.

Roland's group, on the other hand, wasn't as lucky...

They had stayed up all night in case any monsters or wild beasts tried getting the jump on them, and had ended up getting eaten alive by mosquitoes and aching all over after getting through the night with only a single blanket. Carrying blankets just meant more things for them to lug around, so one was their limit. It would have been a different story if they could just leave the old ones behind and buy more at the towns they encountered along the way, but they didn't have that particular luxury.

They had cold meat skewers they'd bought from a food stall for dinner last night, and breakfast was hardtack.

Seeing that Kaoru had taken off, they hurried to follow after her.

"Do they seem like they're getting faster, Sir Roland?"

Just as Francette said, they were certainly faster than yesterday.

"...Is she getting better?"

That was exactly what was happening. She was using potions, not only to fix the pain in her joints, but to strengthen them, as well. To top it all off, she was getting personal lessons from the very horse she was riding.

"Raise your waist a little bit more. Yup, just like that. Try and get a feel for the way my body moves while running. Clamp your knees a bit tighter against me, too... Yeah, that's the way."

He was there to teach her the riding techniques that the soldiers used and to give her advice on how to make riding easier for her, so of course she was getting better. Ed was one of the elite, a horse selected for the vanguard and given extra water even when the rest of the empire's troops were suffering. On top of all that, Kaoru herself was light—lighter than Roland or any of the others following along with him. Compared to full-grown guys in armor carrying swords, it was like she weighed nothing at all.

Every time they took a break, Ed and Kaoru would down a healing potion together. Roland's group, on the other hand, was weighed down with camping gear, food, and water, making it steadily more difficult to keep up with Ed.

"This isn't good, Sir Roland! At this rate, she's just going to keep putting more distance between us!"

"Even if we force the horses to run faster to keep up, they're going to be exhausted in no time at all! We haven't been giving them enough water as it is!"

"There's no point if she gets away from us now!"

Though they'd somehow managed to keep up with her yesterday, she was moving at a much faster pace today. Things could get entirely out of hand by tomorrow.

It was then that Francette came in and offered a suggestion of her own:

"Let's split up into two groups. One group will make camp near Kaoru and keep up with her until around noon, while the other will travel about half a day ahead. While they won't get to sleep any later than usual, they'll be able to rest easy until the next morning. Come afternoon, they'll take over following Kaoru from the other morning team, who will be able to take their time as they continue along until they reach the campsite. When they do, the night team will set out again. Then we repeat this pattern from there."

"Nice thinking! That's not a bad plan at all. How should we split ourselves up then?"

"I believe you and I are best suited to handle the nighttime shift. If anything were to happen, there's a much higher chance of it being at night, after all. I imagine it would be much easier that way, since I serve directly under you, and having a girl with you should make it easier to approach Kaoru. In terms of fighting prowess, having the two of us in one group and four royal guards in the other should also be a fairly even way of splitting up our fighting power, as well."

With that said, however, in her heart of hearts, Francette was fidgeting around sheepishly. She didn't know if it was an angel or the Goddess who had put such a wonderful idea in her head, but whoever it was, she couldn't thank them enough.

As I continued along my journey and chatted with Ed, there was one thing that was bothering me...

He's way too smart... How is a horse able to talk normally with me? Were horses always this smart, and we just never knew, since they couldn't talk with us?

No, that was totally out of the question. So could it be that Ed was actually only as smart as a baby, but my auto-translating ability was making it easier for me to understand? Or was my ability to understand all languages forcibly putting him on a level where he could talk normally with me?

No, that can't be it, either...

Even if we assumed horses had roughly the same knowledge as a three-year-old, they still wouldn't be as smart as dogs. That was the response most jockeys in Japan gave when asked in a questionnaire. If that were the case, then the comparison just wouldn't make sense.

And if we were going that far, did horses even have anything you could call a "language" in the first place? Same goes for that squirrel-thing I got directions from after I first got here...

I had a feeling I wasn't ever going to find the answer, no matter how much I thought it over, so I just gave up on that particular train of thought. So long as we could understand each other, that was good enough for me. It was way better than not being able to understand him at all.

While Kaoru and Ed were having a pleasant time on their trip, Roland and his group certainly couldn't say the same for themselves. Up till now, they'd always been able to restock their food and water from whatever town or village they'd happened to pass through last before "roughing" it outside, in the loosest sense of the word.

Though Roland may have been royalty, he'd also received military training, and had as much experience camping out in the wilderness as everyone else. His experience with camping, however, was with a proper campsite being set up, being able to eat hot meals, and sleeping in a simple bed with plenty of blankets. He hadn't ever slept on a straw mat like the lower-class soldiers or anything.

For normal soldiers, it would take around seven or eight days of marching to reach the front. Since Kaoru was traveling by herself and moving faster all the time, however, it would take her about three or four days to get there. That was what Roland and the others had told themselves, in order to get through the harsh job of tailing Kaoru, but it looked like the battlefield was actually further to the west than they'd first thought. By the time they reached anywhere near the fighting, six whole days had passed since they'd first set off...

"Looks like we made it. Let's try heading over there; that's where they set up camp."

"You got it, missy."

Kaoru and Ed set off toward what looked to be a command post set up in the back end of the battlefield. Just as she was expecting, they were immediately stopped by soldiers when they got close.

"Who are you supposed to be?!" A group of soldiers surrounded Kaoru as they challenged her to identify herself.

"Me? My name's Kaoru. Would you happen to need healing potions, by chance?"

"Huh?"

There wasn't anyone among the soldiers here who had seen Kaoru up close and personal like this before, so they had no idea who she was, since she'd used her own name instead of introducing herself as an "angel" or "a friend of the Goddess."

They had, however, heard the rumors about the healing potions. They weren't exactly the most expensive thing in the world, but they were just pricey enough that they hadn't had a chance to use one themselves. They'd heard testimonials from people who had, though. Having those with them would be an absolute boon out on the battlefield.

But the girl in front of them was empty-handed, and they weren't quite sure what to do with her.

While the soldiers were struggling with how to handle the situation, Roland and his group came rushing over to them at that exact moment. The other four royal guards had turned back and set up camp after finding the Balmore troops, and had already regrouped with Roland and Francette that morning.

"My name is Roland. I want you to take me to the general."

There wasn't a single soldier who didn't know of the king's brother. After hastily saluting him, they did as he asked and led him to the general's tent.

"Sir Roland! What the heck would bring you all the way out here?!" General Menes, the commander in charge of the troops, reacted in shock as he met with Roland's group.

"I'm sorry for coming out of the blue like this. Let's just say I had my own...'reasons' for coming. How's the situation over here?" Roland asked.

"Yes, sir..." A grimace clouded the general's face in response to Roland's question. "With the second wave of about 20,000 soldiers having made it over the mountains, the enemy forces number roughly 40,000 after joining their comrades. Our forces have managed to stop their advance, with mostly small skirmishes here and there between us so far. We're moving as fast as we can to return to the capital and provide reinforcements, but the enemy advances if we pull back, and pulls back if we try to advance on them. It's an obvious bid for time on their part. If we tried to go on the offensive and make an aggressive push, on the other hand, it would only lead to more losses on our part. Not only that, but if things go bad, there's the risk we won't be able to return to support the troops at the capital."

The general held the same despondent look on his face as he recounted his troops' struggles. That was when Roland gave him the good news.

"Not to worry. We've already captured the 20,000 enemy troops who arrived from Rueda, and our own troops are unharmed. We have 15,000 troops protecting the capital right now. There's no need to worry about Grua, so focus all your efforts on taking care of the enemy in front of you."

"YEEEEEEAAAHHH!!!"

The sound of cheers filled the commander's tent.

"I-Is that really true?!"

"Do I have any reason to lie?"

"Then that means we can fight more freely, and we won't have to push our soldiers any more than we need to!" General Menes was practically shaking with joy.

"So…" Kaoru butted in after staying silent all this time. "What would happen if the enemy realized their other forces that had gone through Rueda were already done for?"

Menes turned to Roland, a doubtful look on his face. "And who would this young girl be, Sir Roland?"

Roland gave a forced smile. "This here is Kaoru…but maybe it'd be easier for you to recognize her if I called her 'a friend of the Goddess.'"

"Oh... Oh my..." The general's eyes went wide.

"So, about my question..." Kaoru sulkily continued.

Seeing how Kaoru wasn't in the best of moods, the general hurried to answer her.

"If they were to find out, then there'd be no need for them to try and stall for time any longer. Their only options would be to pull back or break through our ranks by force. There's almost no chance they'd retreat, though..."

"Why's that?"

"Even if they retreated, there's nothing left for the empire. The only way for Aligot to continue growing is to invade other countries. If they were to lose this many soldiers in their invasion and then retreat, then it would take decades for them to make another attempt. The other countries around them would be on much higher alert, building up their own militaries to reduce Aligot's power. That we know about their backroom deal with Rueda and their ambush through the mountains means they won't be nearly as effective if they try to use the same methods again. If they managed to wipe out our forces here, they'd probably imagine that taking down the troops stationed at the capital shouldn't be much more difficult. It seems they aren't aware of the infusion of soldiers from the east that came as reinforcements to protect Grua. That's why they appear to be underestimating the amount of soldiers we have protecting the royal capital."

Assuming the instigators needed three times as many soldiers, if the defending side had 10,000 troops, the attackers would need 30,000 to take them on. If Aligot thought there were fewer than that guarding the capital, then 30,000 would be plenty. If that was the case, then they'd just have to keep their own casualties to 10,000 or less. Losing roughly a third of your troops in battle was devastating, but losing half of them meant your side had been annihilated.

Most of the time, a battle would be decided right then and there. If Aligot had 30,000 soldiers to spare after beating the enemy here, then the empire should have a good chance of winning this war. Once Aligot laid siege to the capital, it was merely a matter of time before the capital surrendered after running out of food and water. They'd take what they needed from the nearby town and request supplies from Rueda if they needed them.

It wouldn't be strange for them to think their victory was assured, if they could just surround the capital, especially for soldiers of a country who took pride in their own military strength.

"It's still going to take some time for the troops here to realize that their comrades to the north were defeated. Who knows how many days it will take for a messenger to travel back through Rueda to deliver the news to Aligot, then go through the mountain path to inform the troops here…"

"Then how about we just tell them ourselves?" Kaoru asked back.

"I doubt they'd believe something the enemy told them so easily…" the general said with a bitter smile.

After thinking it over, a sinister smile crossed Kaoru's face.

"Then let's give them some bait they won't be able to ignore!"

Oh boy, here we go again… Roland thought to himself as he caught a glimpse of Kaoru's face.

The next morning, a message rang through the air to the Balmore soldiers fighting on the front line.

"Listen up, and listen good! His Highness, Sir Roland has arrived from the royal capital, and he's brought news that the enemy forces entering through Rueda have been crushed, as well as plenty of healing potions for everyone! None should worry about their injuries! For those already injured or sick, be sure you get yours as soon as you can!"

The words rang out far and wide in all directions, reaching not only the enemy soldiers, but their superior officers as well.

Chapter 13:
A Divine Blade

That same day, the Aligot forces suddenly went on an all-out offensive.

"Seems like your name had quite an impact, Sir Roland. Who knows if they want to take you down for glory, or just take you hostage, but having you say we defeated the army that came through Rueda made it all the more credible."

There were a mix of emotions on Roland's face when he heard Kaoru's words.

Kaoru, Roland, and the others were on a raised hill near the front lines, standing out plain as day while on horseback—all on purpose, of course.

The front lines were already embroiled in melee combat as both armies clashed against each other. If Kaoru were to use all the powers she had at her disposal, she might have been able to reduce the amount of soldiers who died in the battle...but what would have happened if she did?

It would have been an overwhelming victory for them with the power of the Goddess on their side. There was no honor in winning like that, and neither the winners nor the losers would be satisfied with that sort of outcome. There'd be no solace for the families of the soldiers who'd died in battle.

Kaoru had come here fully intending to wield her powers as much as she could, but it wasn't to help one army completely destroy the other in a one-sided battle. It was to keep casualties to a minimum for each side and bring this whole war to a speedy conclusion. She was merely waiting for her most opportune chance to intervene.

"Hey, Sir Roland. Start going around and acting like a complete weirdo, if you please," said Kaoru.

"…And why would I do that, exactly?" Roland answered, not looking particularly enthused by her request.

"If you start acting suspicious all of a sudden, it should make the enemy worried that their prey is going to make a run for it, or maybe try to do something unplanned for. It should be enough to make them look your way every once in a while to check on you. While they're distracted with you, it should put our own soldiers at an advantage."

"…All right, fine."

Roland began wandering around aimlessly, occasionally waving at no one in particular, all for the sake of the soldiers. He was a fine example of what a superior officer should be.

After some time had passed, there was an obvious change in the enemy's tactics. Instead of focusing on other, much more essential areas to attack, they'd begun sending their troops at the small hill Kaoru and Roland were on. Several soldiers on horseback spearheaded the charge, with countless other foot soldiers following behind them. They couldn't have brought horses with them over the mountains, so they had probably acquired the horses from local sources.

"All right, looks like they took the bait. Let's wait for them to get a bit closer before you lead them straight into the ambush we've set up for them. I'm going to get myself a better spot to watch it all go down."

The hill had no actual influence on the battle, and would have been completely ignored under all other circumstances. If it wasn't for the fact that there was such tantalizing bait being dangled in front of them here, this spot would have no strategic value whatsoever. It'd just be a spot with a harmless-looking girl, and thus not worth redirecting soldiers to send over there.

"...I know," Roland said as he stared at the soldiers advancing upon them.

The squad of enemy soldiers cut a swath through the Balmore troops in their way, getting even closer to Kaoru and Roland. They looked to be a group of Aligot's most elite, so they must have made capturing Roland one of their top priorities. The balance of troops on the field had broken after Aligot redeployed soldiers for this attack, allowing the Balmore forces to gain the upper hand.

Everything was going according to plan. All that was left now was to lead them into their ambush and surround them, annihilating those forces and reducing Aligot's presence on the battlefield.

"It's almost showtime. Make sure they get a good look at you out there."

"I know..." Roland answered back. He raised his hand as high as he could to draw attention to himself before shouting out his next order. "We're heading down there! Everyone, follow after me!"

He descended the hill, gradually moving in a direction without any friendly Balmore troops to make it easier for the enemy to follow him.

"Now then, time to wait and see how this all plays out…"

Wars in this world were by no means quick affairs. The battle had only just begun, and it'd still be some time before Kaoru would step in—maybe even a few days, at that.

It wasn't a good feeling watching others engage in a battle to the death, but this was war. Only the most foolhardy of optimists would think this would be resolved without anyone dying.

While Kaoru was hanging back and waiting for the action to unfold, Ed hesitantly spoke up.

"…*Hey, little missy.*"

"What's up?"

"*It might just be me here…but is the enemy totally ignoring the bait and coming straight for us?*"

"…Uh-oh."

The Aligot soldiers had received very specific orders on who to capture. Their top priority was the girl said to have received the blessing of the Goddess, the one who had the ability to make healing potions. Their second highest priority was anyone from the royal family, and their third priority was any cabinet minister or high-ranking aristocrat. They were free to ignore the other targets if it meant securing their number one priority, even if it meant losing massive numbers of troops in the process.

They'd even received word about what the girl in question looked like: around ten to twelve years old, black hair and black eyes, and a cute face, with a harsh glare in her eyes. And who else had arrived alongside Roland, the brother of Balmore's king, but a little girl who matched that very description? She'd not only brought with her an abundance of healing potions, but was even going so far as to stand on the front lines of the battlefield.

The elite squad of soldiers that had broken off from the main army wasn't going for Roland, but for Kaoru. Not only that, but for some reason, Roland and the other troops had left that girl all on her own as they headed off somewhere. There was no better chance than this, and they weren't about to pass it up.

"Crap… They've got me surrounded."

The soldiers rushed to form a circle around Kaoru so she wouldn't be able to get away on horseback. They took advantage of Kaoru panicking over what to do, not giving her any time to figure out her next step. They managed to form a semi-circle behind her, gradually closing in as they made the circle tighter.

The group of soldiers in front of her were coming in closer and closer…

"Oh crap, oh crap, oh crap! You think you can get us out of here, Ed?!"

"That's a no-can-do, missy!"

Well, can't say I saw this one coming… Should I go with an explosion here…? No, there's no point in doing that. All I'd end up with is a bunch of dead bodies on my hands. I may be able to kill a few off with poison, but there's too many to take them all on… What should I do? Make an explosion big enough to create an escape route? But they might start firing off arrows if I try to run away… I think I might actually die if one of those hits me. I'm pretty sure they're not going to kill me if they catch me. There should be plenty of chances to escape…

While Kaoru was wrestling over what to do next, the circle of Aligot soldiers had steadily closed in on her to try and capture her unharmed. She couldn't break through them, since they had their swords and spears pointed solely at her. Several of them had even

107

sheathed their swords and moved closer to drag Kaoru down off her horse.

Right when Kaoru found herself out of options and unable to figure out what move to take next, the Aligot soldiers on horseback suddenly changed direction.

"Is that…Francette?"

Francette had turned around after realizing something was wrong, Roland and four other royal guards desperately chasing after her.

The soldiers didn't stand a chance. They were up against Francette, a veritable demon of a warrior; Roland, the valiant brother of the king of Balmore; and a group of the most elite warriors that the kingdom could provide. This wasn't a combination the makeshift Aligot cavalry could handle.

Francette and the others broke through the enemy soldiers surrounding Kaoru, dismounting from their horses and forming up around her.

Everyone was more than capable of fighting on horseback, but their main area of expertise was doing battle on foot. Being on horseback usually gave you the advantage in a fight, but when it came to truly skilled soldiers such as themselves, they found that horses just weren't able to keep up with them. Being surrounded by soldiers while on a horse meant that they wouldn't be able to protect themselves against any attacks made from their rear, or from the side where they weren't holding their weapon. Dealing with multiple enemies at the same time was nearly impossible, as well. On top of that, having someone they needed to protect meant keeping the fight on the ground was their only choice.

"Sorry… Looks like I screwed up here," Kaoru said, disheartened.

The six people who'd rushed to her aid laughed it off, saying that it was about time they had a chance to show what they could do.

Thus marked the beginning of their fierce struggle. Roland and the other four royal guards were all brandishing short swords as they charged into battle. Despite their name, they weren't any shorter than the average sword or anything. Soldiers on horseback generally carried longswords, while foot soldiers went with short swords. That they used them just proved that they weren't merely cavalry.

Though short swords were usually wielded with one hand, Roland and his men were using both, since they didn't have shields to carry. Even without shields, they just had to block any strikes coming their way with the sword itself. Hack, parry, stab, slash, repeat.

Unlike a katana, these blades weren't for slicing clean through people. They would overpower their opponent by force, crushing them beneath the blade. They still had enough of an edge to them to lop off a limb, though.

Francette, on the other hand, had a bastard sword as her weapon of choice. It was a sword that could be wielded with either one or two hands, but was much heavier and longer than a shortsword. It wasn't the type of weapon a girl who looked to be in her mid-teens should be able to handle—under normal circumstances, that is. It should go without saying that Francette's circumstances were anything but normal.

Her sword would drag along the ground if she tried to wear it on her hip like normal, so she usually had it strapped on her back. Though she wanted to use an even larger and heftier sword to put her tremendous strength to use, her size meant that it was impossible for her to carry anything larger than she had now.

Francette swung her bastard sword with all the grace and finesse of one wielding an epee in fencing, gleefully mowing down any enemy soldier who had the poor fortune of standing before her. Screams of agony and pain filled the air as the piles of corpses and injured grew in the wake of her warpath.

"I-It's…Fearsome Fran…" the Aligot soldiers whispered, their voices trembling in fear.

The Balmore forces who had been lying in wait for the ambush realized the plan had gone awry, and began cutting their way through the enemy lines, ultimately surrounding the enemy on both sides to eliminate them. Chaos and confusion dominated the fight as the battle raged on. There was only one thing that both sides were clear on: do *not* harm the girl.

The fight had devolved into such chaos that there wasn't anything else Kaoru could do. Using her nitroglycerin potions or any other sort of chemical attack would just get her allies caught up in the blast radius. She could try using her Item Box powers here, but that would ruin the story she had been pushing so far, the one where she was a normal human who just so happened to be friends with the Goddess.

But I guess the same thing would happen if I started making everything explode, huh…

With the number of fallen enemy soldiers reaching triple digits, Kaoru breathed a sigh of relief knowing that, even though she was in the middle of a battlefield, she was at least safe for now…

That's when it happened.

Roland had managed to deflect an arrow with the right shoulder of his armor to protect one of his allies, but his sword had stopped moving in the process. An Aligot soldier thrust their own sword forward, not one to let this chance slip them by.

The sound of metal clashing against metal rang out through the battlefield. Francette had lost her balance from overextending to deflect the attack, gripping the shattered remains of her sword. It was already at its limit from taking the brunt of Francette's monstrous strength, but forcing that slash had finally caused the blade to give in.

Taking full advantage of this perfect chance, the enemy had plunged a single spear deep into the right side of her chest. Fresh blood spurted from the newly carved hole as the spear was ripped out of her.

"Fran!!!" Roland caught Francette before she could hit the ground.

"I-I did it! I took down Fearsome Fran!!" the Aligot soldier cheered.

The next instant, his head exploded into countless tiny pieces.

"Don't gimme that crap..."

The blood had rushed to Kaoru's head. Any thought of trying to keep to her story about being a normal girl had been pushed from her mind.

While she was the same girl who had said she didn't care if soldiers died, since that was their job, the moment she saw the spear pierce Francette's chest and the blood spurting from her wound... nothing else mattered anymore.

It was different than watching countless soldiers dropping like flies. Once it was someone she was fond of, that's what made the difference. She knew how contradictory she was being but, despite that, she couldn't stop her blood from boiling.

She patted Ed's neck. He didn't need her to say anything to know what that meant. He knelt down, letting Kaoru off his back.

111

The Aligot troops around them had gone dead silent. Though they may have gotten used to the blood from their enemies splattering on them, it seemed they weren't exactly used to the same thing happening with the brain matter from their comrade's head exploding.

The stillness was only momentary, however. The sounds of fighting still raged on all around them.

Kaoru turned her gaze skyward. The next instant, the thunderous roar of an explosion ripped through the battlefield. It could have been the work of the Goddess, or the work of a devil…or maybe even an omen of a catastrophe to come.

The booming explosion that rocked the battlefield had brought the fighting to a halt. A pillar of golden clouds had formed around Kaoru, as if to show exactly where the sound had come from.

Then she shouted for all to hear:

"I'm about to go through with an important ceremony, so you all just shut up and watch! If you want to keep fighting, then do it the hell after!"

Her voice wasn't loud enough to reach the entire battlefield, but it still traveled decently far due to her elevated position. Word would eventually travel to the rest. No one knew what would happen to them if they tried to go against her.

Kaoru took another look in Francette's direction. Though she looked gravely injured, it seemed like she'd be able to hold out a little longer.

Kaoru walked toward her and Roland.

"N-Now's our chance! Quick, grab the ange—"

BANG!

The soldier who tried to move in to capture Kaoru suddenly had his head blown clean off his shoulders. No one else dared move an inch anymore.

Kaoru stopped a few meters away from Francette, the blood from her pierced lungs dribbling from her mouth. Then, in a loud, commanding voice, Kaoru proclaimed to her:

"Francette, your life is the very epitome of what a knight should be. You dedicated everything you had to protecting your lord."

Francette gave a weak, yet satisfied smile as Roland supported her body.

"It's not exactly the most ladylike life for a girl to live, though, is it?"

Francette looked to be in minor shock at such harsh words.

"That is why I shall give you a gift for your next life. What would you like? Better facial features? Glossier hair? Skin as smooth as silk? A bountiful bust? Go ahead, make your choice."

"I…want power… I want the power…to protect Sir Roland… again…" Francette sputtered, blood dripping from her mouth as she used every last ounce of her strength to get the words out.

"…I thought you'd say that," Kaoru said, walking toward Francette again. "It's a foolish request…but one I think you should fulfill in this life, not the next."

With a flick of her wrist, Kaoru was suddenly holding a potion bottle that had appeared out of thin air. Opening the lid, she poured the contents inside Francette's mouth.

"Wh…at…?" Francette couldn't help but let out a gasp of shock as she found all her wounds healed in the blink of an eye.

Kaoru glanced at the remains of Francette's bastard sword. "It seems this particular blade wasn't enough for you."

The next thing in her hand was a sword, seemingly conjured out of thin air like the potion. It was made of a special alloy, one hard enough so it would never break. The edge of the blade was sharpened to a fine point on a molecular level, and it used the bioelectricity of whoever gripped its hilt as an energy source to vibrate the blade at incredibly high speeds.

In short, it was a sort of "vibroblade," a weapon straight out of science fiction. She'd managed to hold herself back from giving it the ability to superheat the blade as well, though.

But how did she suddenly have the power to make swords?

Well…she didn't.

If you twisted the hilt of the weapon, you would find that the inside was full of a healing potion. It was just a container for a potion, shaped to look like a sword.

"You will have the power to create any medicine in any container you are thinking of."

In terms of how brokenly powerful her abilities were, the power to make potions Kaoru had so casually asked Celes for was something that even surpassed her Item Box.

With equal parts awe and reverence, Francette ceremoniously accepted the blade I held out to her. This was no ordinary sword, and everyone who saw what happened knew it.

Wait, I gotta give this thing a name…

I panicked a little when I realized that. I wasn't even thinking about giving it a name when I made it, but I kinda had to after putting on that whole show. The only problem was that nothing good was coming to mind.

If we're thinking of legendary swords, it has to be Excalibur, right? No, that's too easy... Maybe Caliburn? No, that's pretty much the same thing... The sword in the stone was supposed to be called Caliburn, and it's often mixed up with Excalibur itself, but that sword was supposed to have been a gift from the Lady of the Lake. There's also a theory that Excalibur is just the improved version of Caliburn. So Excalibur is like an *extra*-strong Caliburn... Wait, extra... Caliburn... Ex-calibur...n. Is that why it's called Excalibur? Hm.

Now that I think about it, Excalibur's sheath was supposed to be even more valuable than the sword itself. Usually you'd make sure the sword had all the bells and whistles, not the sheath. Guess that meant the sheath was made after the sword, then.

Wait, did Excalibur even have a sheath? It was stuck in a rock, so I guess it not having a sheathe made sense. Let's see, what was Excalibur based on in the first place...

All right, let's take a page out of Norse mythology and borrow the name of the sword Sigurd used, then combine that with Arthur's sword to make a name more powerful than either of them alone...

"Francette the Knight: I bestow upon you the title of einherjar, a protector of the Goddess, and grant you the divine blade 'Exgram.' Use it to cut open a path to victory. Now, go, my divine warrior! Go, Francette the Einherjar!"

"*Raaaaaagh!*"

With a spirited war cry, Francette stood up once more, and the war was back on.

Shng!

The newly christened Exgram swung through the air without the slightest hint of resistance. It looked like nothing happened, or maybe that she'd missed—but that was before the upper half of the

Aligot troops slid off their bodies. The swords and armor that tried to defend against it all melted like butter.

"Huh...?"

Friend, enemy, and even the person who swung the sword herself were awestruck by the sharpness of the blade's honed edge.

Heh...

Heheh...

Heheheh...

A demonic smile crossed over Francette's face. She broke off in a sprint toward the enemy troops, showing them the reason she'd earned the nickname "Fearsome Fran."

The screams of the Aligot soldiers echoed across the battlefield...

Roland turned to look at me, eyes full of expectation.

All right, fine. I can't have him dying on me, either.

I reached up into the air and worked my magic.

"Here, this one's called Exridill. I'm going to have to ask you to give this back after the fight's over, though. You're not an einherjar or anything, after all."

"Aw, what? Come on..." Though he made his disappointment known, Roland charged off to join the battle.

Before I knew it, I had the other four royal guards looking at me with the same puppy-dog eyes Roland had been giving me...

Francette sliced anyone close to her into actual ribbons as she cut her way through the battlefield. It was no use trying to block her strikes with their swords, since they'd just end up cleaved in half as well. Even if they managed to get in one good strike on her in exchange for sacrificing their own soldiers, she'd just be brought back to life again—and probably even stronger the next time. There was no way they could win against that.

So they ran. They ran away as fast as their legs would take them, not caring one bit about keeping up appearances...and with Francette in hot pursuit.

Not having friendly troops nearby made things easier for her, since she didn't have to worry about them getting caught up in her warpath. She was free to swing Exgram, the legendary weapon that would become her trusty blade from this day forth, to her heart's content. Though Francette had already gone beyond the realm of normal humans the day she drank the potion Kaoru gave her, the giddiness she felt after obtaining a power even beyond that had her shaking with joy.

The enemy... I have to get somewhere with more targets.

Francette took off in a mad dash, completely forgetting about the person she was supposed to be protecting.

Roland desperately chased after Francette. She was a simple girl at heart, and after the spectacle Kaoru had put on to give her the sword, she was completely out of control. He couldn't just leave her alone.

Following after them were the other four royal guards, each with their own divine sword in hand.

The legendary blade, Exhrotti. Just like with Gram and Ridill, Kaoru had borrowed another name from one of the swords Sigurd had used.

She'd told them it was one legendary sword split into four and its power was diminished because of that, but the sharpness of its blade was more than worthy of its legendary status. To tell the truth, it was just a sword she'd put together out of special alloys, and didn't have any super high-frequency vibration functions or anything to it. Still, that should be enough for a group of elite soldiers like them.

No girl could have resisted the four pairs of puppy-dog eyes being turned at her...probably. Well, not this one at least.

The (supposedly) elite Aligot troops screamed bloody murder, turning tail and running for dear life—with one war-crazed berserker laughing as she chased after them.

The fleeing Aligot soldiers didn't have a chance of outrunning her. She cut them down one after the other, laughing maniacally all the while.

"F-Fearsome Fran has a divine blade!"

"Sh-She was on the brink of death, but she's alive again! And she's even stronger than before!"

"That angel isn't human! She's on the same level as the Goddess herself! We should have never tried to lay hands on her!"

The explosion in the sky, the angel's solemn warning, and now, the one mad warrior sowing death and destruction wherever she went, with five other grim reapers following behind her...

The screams of their fleeing allies in their ears, the other Aligot soldiers were frozen in terror. Unable to fight against that fear any longer, one soldier slowly backed away, eventually turning around and making a straight dash away from the front lines. Another soldier followed after the first, then more and more after them, until the Aligot troops were fleeing en masse.

The front lines of the Aligot troops crumbled. Francette hunted down the fleeing soldiers, while Roland and the other royal guards cut down any stragglers who managed to escape her wrath.

"We've already come this far, so this is pretty much what was going to happen anyway," Kaoru muttered to herself. "If that's the

119

case, then it'd be better to end this quickly and keep the amount of casualties to a minimum. Since Francette and the others are the ones making the empire turn tail and run, you can even say this is a victory for the soldiers of Balmore."

With that, she turned her attention to a spot just beyond the front lines, one that had nothing but Aligot soldiers gathered there. Aiming for the sky just above them, she created two gourd-shaped glass containers out of thin air. She'd filled one full of pseudo-nitroglycerin and the other with concentrated sulfuric acid, bringing them together to create one enormous explosion. And then another… Then a third.

Next thing she did was create a vast array of small glass balls in the sky filled with her pseudo-nitroglycerin. They fell down one after the other, leaving a sea of explosions in their wake.

She'd tried picking a spot without too many people around, but that didn't work out exactly as planned. A good number of Aligot soldiers ended up dying after being caught up in the blasts.

Now it wasn't just the front lines turning tail and running, but the soldiers behind them, and the reserve troops even further behind running for dear life. There was only one thought going through their minds: *"We pissed off the Goddess!"*

Even if it had been fifty-three years since she last appeared, the Goddess wasn't just a legend here—she was a reality. Some elderly people had even seen her the last time she descended. Only someone on the same level as the Goddess herself could cause a phenomenon such as this.

While the explosions could have been caused by devils or demons, the existence of the girl who was said to be a messenger and friend of the Goddess meant it wasn't likely. The way she'd conferred

Fearsome Fran with her own divine blade was like reenacting something out of a legend.

One of the soldiers who'd escaped Francette's wrath managed to make it back to the commanding officers of the western invasion forces. Expressions of despair covered their faces when they heard what was going on. They'd all thought she was nothing more than a little girl who was able to create potions thanks to the grace of the Goddess.

All this time, the Aligot forces had been under the impression that *they* would be on the Goddess's good side if they could get the girl to the pope in Rueda and have him talk things over with her. Anyone who opposed them was opposing the Goddess herself. As far as the empire was concerned, Balmore just happened to be the place the girl had decided to settle down. She'd already had an open feud with the temple and the royal family before, after all.

But now she'd not only brought about a miracle in reviving one of the Balmore warriors from the brink of death, and granted her a legendary weapon in the process, but she'd even doled out divine punishment to their soldiers. Forget about trying to persuade her; they couldn't even try and capture her at this rate. If anyone tried to get close to her, their head would explode in a shower of red mist. Who'd be insane enough to try and capture someone like that?

She wasn't just some girl who had received a blessing from the Goddess, but was someone who *handed out* blessings, instead. That being the case, she either worked directly under the Goddess, or maybe she was a goddess herself...

They'd thought Balmore was plotting something when Balmore troops began shouting about potions and Roland and how the invading force to the north was defeated. But now they'd seen what happened with Francette, so it might all be true. It was hard to believe that Balmore had wiped out their forces to the north without taking any losses themselves, but it wasn't impossible if they'd met their end because of divine punishment.

For now, their only option was to retreat. Though they hadn't lost that many soldiers in the fighting, their numbers were still fewer than Balmore's.

But that wasn't the real reason why they chose to back off. Rather, morale was at an all-time low. They'd angered the Goddess, and divine punishment had been delivered unto them as a result. If they angered her any more than they already had, all of them were going to face punishment from on high and get sent straight to hell. Their families back home would be killed as well, and their entire country would perish. They couldn't keep it together and fight with all that on their minds.

Besides, they'd more than fulfilled their mission of keeping the bulk of Balmore's army away from the capital. If Balmore had been lying, then the northern troops would lay siege to the capital and bring it down.

Even if Balmore's main forces returned now, they'd have no choice but to surrender if the capital fell. In fact, the *whole country* would have no choice.

And what if the northern forces really had been wiped out? The answer: they didn't know. That was the responsibility of the general in charge of those troops, not theirs. It didn't have anything to do with the western invasion forces.

But they only had just shy of 40,000 troops with them. Not only were they outnumbered by their enemy, they barely had any heavy armor or mounted troops after being forced to trek through the mountains. Who knew if they'd be able to take the heavily fortified capital after being forced to march there on the limited provisions they could acquire from the villages they'd passed along the way?

They would have to rely on the precious few resources the laborers they'd brought with them carried, and then keep looting whatever they could find as they moved on ahead. It was an uphill battle, even under normal circumstances, but everyone's morale having plummeted certainly didn't help. They would have to rally and rein in the troops that had fled, lighting a fire under them so they would keep fighting as the wrath of the Goddess rained down on them.

...It would never work.

They wouldn't be able to retreat at that point, and they'd lose every single soldier who'd set foot in Balmore, the northern forces included. The only soldiers left would be the 20,000 left on standby in Aligot as a deterrent for if Aseed ever decided to attack them while most of their army was absent. It would mean the end of the empire if that happened.

If enough time passed, Aseed and Brancott would just end up sending reinforcements to aid Balmore. Both countries knew that if Balmore fell, they'd be next. In fact, it wouldn't be strange if Aseed was to start sending troops in a surprise attack from the south right around now.

The commanding officers thought it over long and hard but, in the end, they already knew the answer from the beginning. They just needed a little extra time to accept it themselves.

"We need to fall back."

Everyone present nodded silently in response. Even before the order was given, the troops had already been moving westward, back from whence they came, but it was an order they still needed to announce. They were still an army, after all.

In the end, the Aligot forces had finally reached the base of the mountain path, all the while taking a severe beating from Balmore's fierce counterattack. They ditched whatever heavy equipment they had with them and disappeared into the craggy mountainside, fleeing back to their own country. The 40,000 they'd marched in with had now been reduced to about 30,000. They'd lost a quarter of their troops in the carnage, and had barely managed to avoid being declared annihilated.

Assuming the remaining soldiers taken prisoner after the failed northern invasion actually made it back home, that meant the empire would have lost around 12,000 troops in this war. That was fifteen percent of Aligot's combined force of 80,000 soldiers. The northern forces had been captured, while the western forces had fled for their lives. No matter how many they lost, it didn't change the fact that this war had ended up in a complete and utter defeat for them.

Afterward, the emperor of Aligot had requested that Rueda negotiate favorable terms of surrender on their behalf, since Rueda was supposed to be a neutral country. They tried framing it as an unfortunate accident on Aligot's part, mainly due to a misunderstanding, in an attempt to try and rekindle whatever favor they once held with Balmore. Instead, Rueda was recognized as an enemy country for having allied with Aligot, and a country that had lost in the war, at that. As such, they were excommunicated from the religion of the Goddess, and lost any shred of authority they once held as a religious power. Suffice it to say, they were in shock.

Chapter 14:
Peace Talks

It had been thirty days since the last of the Aligot soldiers had disappeared through the mountain pass they'd come from. A conference to negotiate terms for peace was going to be held in Grua. There weren't any neutral countries that could serve as the host for the talks, and since it had been such a one-sided victory on Balmore's part, the talks were going to be held on the victor's home soil.

The war had not only involved Aligot as the aggressor, but the Holy Land of Rueda as well, the spiritual center of the religion of the Goddess. Spectators had gathered, not only from the countries involved in the war, but from Balmore's allies in Aseed and Brancott, and even people from countries of influence on the mainland further east of Brancott.

The central plaza of the royal capital of Balmore was chosen to host the talks. It was a wide area, located just between the main temple and the front gates of the palace.

It was unprecedented to have peace talks held out in the open for all to see, but that was because it would have been too much to ask to try and cram everyone into a single room. For some reason, the representatives from Rueda were also pushing to have this held outdoors, which was why a special stage had been built in the center of the plaza.

There were plenty of influential people in attendance, but most were only there to listen, not speak. The only ones participating in these talks would be Balmore, Aligot, and Rueda, with the chance of asking Aseed their opinion on certain matters, since they shared a border with Aligot as well.

Everyone from Balmore was calm and composed. Not only were they not at fault, since they were the ones who had been invaded, they had ended up victorious, as well.

The representatives from Aligot, on the other hand, were absolutely pale in comparison...

Strangely enough, the group from Rueda was entirely unfazed, despite how awful the situation should have been for them.

With the representatives from all the various countries watching intently, the peace conference officially started.

To start, the Balmore side gave a brief overview of how the war had played out. They demanded reparations from the Aligot Empire for their aggression, a ransom for the prisoners of war they'd taken, as well as compensation for things like food and medical costs, where Balmore had already taken care of them. To top it off, they demanded Aligot make a vow of non-aggression, as well. If they were to break that, after the representatives from all the different countries had witnessed it, then they'd all come together to gang up on Aligot.

With their country's finances already in dire straits, having to pay the exorbitant price Balmore demanded would be the final nail in the coffin for the empire.

"Balmore is the reason this war happened in the first place! They took the angel hostage and had a monopoly on her miraculous healing potions. The fault lies with them! Our country was only trying to save her!" Aligot's prime minister desperately argued. Kaoru, however, casually brushed aside his assertions.

"I'm not really an 'angel,' you know? I just happened to end up here after wandering around from country to country. I sell potions to everyone, whether they're from Aseed, Brancott, Rueda, or otherwise. Why didn't Aligot just pay for some as well?"

"B-But they wouldn't arrive in time, because of the expiration date…"

"I mean, yeah, not much you can do about that. An expiration date is an expiration date, after all. You wouldn't be too happy if Balmore declared war on you if they weren't able to get your fresh fish delivered in time, right?"

"…"

Kaoru had effortlessly shut down the prime minister's counterargument.

"But, that said, you may have a point. I'll work on fixing the expiration date to make sure they can make it to Aligot in time."

"Wh… What…?"

"And I know that trying to pay all this compensation to Balmore is going to bankrupt your country, but I might have a way to help you with that. Would you care to hear me out?"

That was when Kaoru revealed to them the shocking truth: There was an enormous island out in the sea, west of Aligot's borders, that rivaled the empire itself in terms of size. It was overflowing with natural and mineral resources. Seafaring was a completely undeveloped field right now, and Aligot had an overwhelming advantage over the other countries, since they were closest to the ocean. They couldn't have a monopoly on it, but Balmore was willing to let them have a go at it, should they want to send an expedition to find the island.

The truth of the matter was that Kaoru had been worried Aligot would be desperate after being pushed into a corner like this. She'd created a healing potion in the shape of the world of Verny to get a better handle on the geography around here. She could see all the rivers and other types of hidden resources on this special globe, since that was exactly how she had wanted it when she thought it up. She wouldn't tell them exactly where all these resources were hidden, though, because that would just be *too* kind of her.

Tears were streaming down the prime minister's face, and everyone from Aligot had left their seats to kneel before her. The spectators from the other countries couldn't believe what they were hearing.

It was almost a given that the empire would be reassigning most of their soldiers into shipbuilding and retraining them as sailors, all in order for them to find new lands yet undiscovered. If they could get enough ships out to sea, they could spread out beyond the continent and start up trade with countries farther away from them. She didn't know the particulars about how to build ships or anything, but she could at least draw them a sketch and let them know the basics they'd need to get the ship's rigging put together.

A fire burned in their eyes after hearing Kaoru say as much. If anyone could do it, it would be the empire. They'd *show* everyone they could do it.

The representatives from the other countries, on the other hand, were in a panic over losing their chance to jump in on this veritable treasure island.

"M-Miss Kaoru, um…do you think we could have some of those blueprints as well?"

"Balmore is already going to get yearly payments from Aligot while they pay off their reparations. It's not good to get too greedy."

Crestfallen, the representative who spoke up drooped his head as he placed both hands on the table in front of him.

All the representatives from the other countries were itching to get back home and start getting their own ships ready, but theirs weren't built for long voyages at sea. They'd need to work on building a brand-new type of ship if they wanted to make that dream a reality.

It was at this moment that the people on both sides of the negotiations who had doubts about Kaoru, and the rumors surrounding her, finally began realizing just how valuable she really was...

Balmore wasn't trying to force the citizens of the Aligot Empire starve to death or anything, which was why they were going to allow the empire to pay off the reparations in installments. Aligot jumped at the chance, seeing a ray of hope for their future, now that they weren't going to end up completely bankrupt trying to pay what they owed.

With the Aligot side looking much better than they did at the start of the talks, it was now time to deal with the Holy Land of Rueda.

Rueda was optimistic about their position here. They'd already had their own ace in the hole prepared from the beginning and, after seeing how well Aligot had been treated, they believed they could make a comeback as well.

Unlike the empire, which had entrusted full diplomatic authority to their prime minister, the pope of Rueda himself was in attendance, even though the negotiations could have been handled by a single cardinal.

"Rueda has cast aside their position as a neutral country and lent their support to Aligot. As an enemy who assisted in the invasion of our country, we demand reparations as well."

"Those are nothing but baseless rumors. Our country remained neutral! We never aided the empire in any way!" one of the cardinals shot back, vehemently denying the claims laid against them.

In response, Balmore presented their corroborating points one after the other. Not only had they not warned Balmore of Aligot's invasion, but the messenger they sent to suggest Kaoru had escaped had arrived suspiciously fast, considering the circumstances. They were under orders to take her away by force if she refused, and if they wanted proof, they could bring out the cardinal who'd tried to do just that. That wasn't to mention the cardinals and priests they'd captured along with the northern invasion forces, who they could also bring here at a moment's notice.

There were also the secret agreements between Rueda and the empire that Balmore had learned of by interrogating Aligot officers.

The other countries had received missives from Balmore, each stating how Rueda had betrayed the Goddess and had been excommunicated because of it, but weren't aware of the particulars until now. The representatives present lashed out with criticism and condemnation against Rueda's actions.

"We know nothing of what you claim. We demand that you immediately withdraw such remarks and apologize for the dissemination of such insulting, slanderous rumors, which do not contain an ounce of truth to them!"

"Isn't that all supposed to be true?" Kaoru responded. "Did the news not get to you guys in Rueda, or are you just hiding it now because it would be inconvenient for you otherwise?"

"H-How *dare* you! You're nothing but a servant of the devil!"

"Oh? Wasn't I supposed to be an angel sent by the Goddess? No matter how many times I denied it, everyone from Rueda just seemed to wanna keep calling me that."

The cardinal's face turned bright red as Kaoru nonchalantly brushed him off.

After staying silent throughout the whole exchange, the pope finally stood up.

"Enough! If it has come to this, then I will use our country's most sacred item to prove that we are in the right! Follower of the devil, you will rue the day you sought to fool the people into thinking yourself an angel! This is the instrument that will spell your doom!" he proclaimed, clutching a crystal sphere in his hand.

"I never claimed to be an angel in the first place. *You* guys were the ones saying that, and I've been denying it this whole time…"

"S-Silence!" the pope roared back, furious that Kaoru was dense enough to not catch on to how impressive he was trying to make himself look. (Kaoru absolutely knew what she was doing, of course.)

The pope pretended like nothing happened as he continued speaking: "This is the very treasure Lady Celestine granted us when she bestowed her miracles upon our country! It is a sacred instrument capable of summoning the Goddess, should our Holy Land ever be threatened!"

So that's why they seemed so confident this whole time… That's probably why they wanted this to be held outside, too.

There would be a great many more witnesses to the Goddess's descent if it were done outdoors, and would leave a bigger impression as well.

Oh boy, I wonder if this is what I think it is…

Something about it had struck a chord with Kaoru.

I'm pretty sure this is one of the things Celes brought up when she was complaining to me. That thing will probably end up doing what he said it would, but not for the reason he's thinking…

"Behold, the miracle of the Goddess! Feast your eyes on the proof that we are the blessed citizens of a great and holy land!"

A brilliant flash erupted from the crystal in his hand. The next moment, a sphere of pure light appeared in the sky above. The sphere gradually changed shape, eventually taking on the form of a resplendently beautiful girl.

The Goddess Celestine had descended.

The pope kneeled down before her, a look of immeasurable joy on his face.

"Where's the distortion?!" Celes roared at him.

"Huh?"

The pope could only stare blankly at the Goddess.

Chapter 15:
The Goddess Descends

"I'm asking you where the distortion is!"

The pope was taken aback by Celestine's menacing attitude. He didn't have a clue what she was talking about, so there was no way he could give her a proper answer.

Kaoru (reluctantly) decided to throw the pope a bone.

"Long time no see, Celes!"

"Kaoru! What are you doing here? Actually, hold that thought, now's not the time for that! There's supposed to be a distortion around here that I didn't pick up on. But where is it?!"

"No, there's no distortion. Those guys over there tried calling you to save their own skins. They keep saying Rueda is some blessed and sacred place, and since they're so much better than everyone else as its chosen people, so everyone has to listen to what they say and not question them. It looks like they called you here to prove that's true," Kaoru explained to Celes, a wry smile on her face.

"What in the world are they talking about?" The face Celes made was something akin to "absolutely disgusted."

"I already told you about those people who got in my way when I was fixing distortions before, remember? It is beyond me why anyone related to them would think they're better than everyone else. I'd say they're even *less* than your average human being, actually. I made them make it up to me by giving them a crystal and telling them to contact me right away if they found a distortion, but now they've decided to use it for their own personal reasons? They even interrupted me doing very important calculations to keep this world in balance just to do it!"

Celes's face was turning redder with every word, righteous fury building inside her.

So that's what she's been doing all this time... Maintaining the world must take more work than I thought.

"I've given out a few dozen of those around the world already. Sometimes I get a few false alarms, but I don't really mind those. Some of the more bizarre natural phenomena or disasters here can certainly seem like they could be distortions, but I'd rather deal with a few false alarms here and there over potentially letting a real one slip by me. What I *do* mind is when people try calling me for their own selfish purposes. This makes the second time in the last few thousand years..."

"W-Wait, would that first time happen to be when I think it was?" Kaoru stammered as she stiffened up.

"Yup, I told you about that, too. I was so angry the last time this happened I ended up destroying a whole country... I couldn't quite find the right way to hold myself back, so I ended up blowing that one up and wrecking the countries around it in the process."

The color drained from everyone's faces when they heard that.

"C-Celes, I'll teach you exactly where Rueda's borders are after this, so let's not get anyone else here involved in your wrath, please..."

"N-No, you can't!" the pope screamed. "Wh-What about the Holy Land of Rueda and her blessed people?!"

"'Holy Land'? 'Blessed people'? I don't think you've been listening, have you? That place was contaminated because of the distortion there, and those people got in my way while I was trying to do my *job* and keep this whole world from being destroyed. If it came down to it, though, I was planning on blowing it up, whether they were in the line of fire or not."

The pope collapsed on the ground when he heard Celes's cold remarks.

"Then, what about the girl? And...is it true we're being excommunicated?"

"I owe Kaoru so much for everything she's done for me. In fact, it's safe to say she's one of my best and most important friends by this point. As for this excommunication business..."

Celes looked up to the sky and pretended to think it over, which was probably her way of going back and sifting through the events that had happened up till now.

"Aha, I see, I see. Well, you seem to be worried about being banned from my religion, but you were never my followers in the first place. You've just been going around using my name without my permission. I've never taught anyone a specific doctrine, and I've never recognized anyone as my follower. I've let you do your own thing, because I thought you were doing everything you could to help others as an apology for getting in my way before. If you people are going to use my name to do evil, however, then I wholly forbid you from using my name ever again. Oh, but if the temples from the other countries have absolutely nothing to do with these people, then you may continue to use my name, *only* if you do so to help others and put them at peace."

Celes's declaration was a death knell for the Holy Land of Rueda. The clergymen of their country had been living in the lap of luxury from the donations they'd swindled out of their followers. Who could say what would happen to them now that the truth was out...?

That's when Kaoru put the final nail in the coffin:

"Hey, don't you think it's weird to keep calling Rueda the Holy Land at this point? I think just plain old Rueda would work from now on."

Everyone present agreed with Kaoru's idea. This was a suggestion from the girl who the Goddess Celestine had not only said she owed a great debt to, but had called a most important friend. Even if Kaoru was just a normal girl, it still would likely have been unanimously approved.

It was hard to tell if the pope and everyone else from Rueda were even breathing anymore...

Celes had lost all interest in them by this point and turned to speak to Kaoru.

"I know you probably haven't done anything since you just arrived, but do you think you're going to have a good time here?" Celes said with a smile.

"I've already been here for a *while*, Celes! Your sense of time is all outta whack! I've gone on *tons* of adventures already, and I've been having plenty of fun!"

"Oh, really? Then I wonder if it's all right to give the other god my first report on how you've been doing."

"Uh... Sure, I don't see why not? If you wait too long, I'll probably end up dying of old age, or some sorta freak accident, here..."

"There's no way that would happen! You tell the funniest jokes, Kaoru," Celes said, giggling.

Did I really say something that funny? Kaoru wondered to herself.

"Then I'll just take a peek at the records and see what I can fill him in on. That should let me know about all the adventures you've been having, too."

Records? What records? Is she talking about that one thing? You know, the thing where, like, everything in the world is recorded? What was it called again...the Acai-Stick records? Has that been keeping tabs on me all this time?

137

Kaoru was getting a little freaked out just thinking about it, so she decided to stop thinking altogether.

"Then I guess I'll get going now. Make sure to enjoy yourself, Kaoru!"

"Oh, wait! About Rueda…"

She just forgot about it, so don't remind her now!!! everyone in the plaza screamed together on the inside.

"Only *some* of them are bad people, so it'd be unfair to punish everyone there because of what happened. I know you must be busy doing your thing, so I'll take care of it for you. Think you can leave it to me?"

"Oh, really? Then I'll do just that. If you see anyone else doing something bad, just do whatever's necessary take care of it."

"Roger that! Good luck getting along with the other god."

"Ehehe~ I'll give it my best shot!"

And with that, Celes disappeared into thin air.

"W-We're saved…"

"I know what you were all thinking back there, but if I just let Celes leave like that, she could've ended up bringing down divine punishment to who *knows* where! She may have ended up taking down this country as well, so that's why I had to make sure and remind her!"

Everyone nodded at Kaoru's explanation, since they knew she was exactly right.

In the end, it wasn't certain what was going on with the reparations and the Holy Land of Rueda—pardon, *just* Rueda. Since the delegation that was supposed to be representing that particular country was now rendered entirely powerless after what had just happened with Celes, there was likely to be a coup there soon enough. They technically hadn't done any sort of damage to Balmore, so they'd probably have to pay for the food used to take care of their prisoners at most. That was why no one seemed particularly concerned about what to do with them.

Since the delegation from Rueda had left without participating in the negotiations, the clergymen that Balmore had captured remained locked in their cells until several months later, when their relatives petitioned for their freedom. Negotiations with Aligot, on the other hand, had proceeded smoothly. After agreeing to pay back their reparations in installments, they wrapped up negotiations for the release of their prisoners, meaning they'd be able to go back to their own country right away.

The representatives from the other countries were going wild. Aseed, Brancott, and the other participants, who'd traveled so far from countries further inland, were deeply moved by having seen the Goddess Celestine in person and having heard her words. What she'd talked about went beyond their wildest dreams, for better or worse. And they'd also found out that the girl with unparalleled knowledge *and* the power to make potions with miraculous abilities *also* happened to be a friend of the Goddess.

She was an incredibly valuable girl, and they knew it. But if they tried anything funny to get her, their entire country would be wiped off the map. She was the friend of a goddess who'd destroy a country just for calling her down for no reason. If they tried doing anything to harm her—no, if they did anything to even *slightly* put her in a bad mood, there was no telling what Celestine would do to them. They'd leave her be, and maybe try asking her for *small* favors. That should probably be the most they could get away with.

For now, each of the representatives agreed to the suggestion of new trade deals with Balmore with the promise of sending delegates from the country to seal the deal sometime in the near future. After deciding that maritime countries should begin building ships, while landlocked countries would focus on speedy delivery for health potions, the meeting was adjourned. Everyone gathered there was finally on their way back to their own countries.

Chapter 16:
A Few Years Later

The years passed by. Kaoru was still the same height, standing at 157 centimeters tall. She had been 158 centimeters when she was twenty-two, so this didn't really come as a shock. Kaoru had thought that she was already this tall when she was this age back on Earth, but was a bit crestfallen to find out that it was all in her head. If 157 centimeters made her look like a twelve-year-old in this world, then 158 centimeters was probably the average for thirteen-year-olds. It could barely be called a change at all.

Kaoru was only thinking of the average height of people in Japan when she'd asked Celes for her new body, so she only had herself to blame for that. The people around her had already realized that this was about as tall as she was going to grow. But Kaoru still held out hope, telling herself that Westerners all loved smaller girls—and also making sure to shove the word "lolicon" deep into the corners of her mind.

Aligot used the designs Kaoru had given them to create a whole new class of ship, establishing a new sea route to the previously undiscovered treasure island of resources to the west of them. They'd focused their efforts into trade routes along the coast, and they were making steady progress in establishing themselves as a maritime nation.

The design Kaoru had offered them was a model ship she'd created using her potion powers, as usual. It was one of the earlier versions of the wooden vessels meant for exploring the open seas. For some reason, the goddess figurehead the empire attached to their boats looked younger than Celestine. The faces they had were definitely cute, but the look they had in their eyes could only be described as "harsh."

The clergymen of Rueda had lost their standing as leaders of the country, and the vast personal fortunes they'd built up over the years were seized by the newly established government. After managing to bring the country relatively under control, they sent a proposal to Balmore asking to be annexed into the kingdom, which Balmore accepted. They were allowed to be governed by their own citizens rather than Balmore's aristocracy, and were treated as a protectorate of the kingdom.

Maybe they'd proposed annexation because they wanted to guarantee the future of their small country after losing their status as the chosen people, or maybe they wanted to be citizens of the same country as Kaoru, since she was a being on the same level as the goddess... Either way, Balmore wasn't going to question their decision.

Even if Aseed didn't stand a chance against Aligot, the new island was about the same distance away for them as it was for Balmore, so they began focusing their efforts on shipbuilding, as well. Not one to take this lying down, Balmore also threw their hat into the ring. They became embroiled in a rivalry with Aseed as each raced against the other for seafaring superiority. Roland came asking for Kaoru's help, but she refused to give anything outside of what she already had for both countries. It wouldn't keep things interesting if she had, after all.

Speaking of Roland, he'd become engaged to none other than Francette, the protector of the Goddess. She was the recipient of a divine blade and was known as a heroine who had saved the country, so there were no qualms about the difference in their social status. There was no one who really could oppose who the royals were allowed to marry or not; on the contrary, the entire country welcomed the idea.

After the proposal, Francette had come before Kaoru to swear undying loyalty to her. While Roland seemed like he was getting up in years now, Francette didn't seem to have changed a bit. Kaoru felt like she'd get told to look in a mirror if she tried bringing it up with Francette, so she'd never tell Francette that, though.

Brancott was beating themselves up over letting a huge catch like her get away. They'd learned that a girl with the power to create potions had appeared at one point in the territory of Baron Renie. Without a doubt, that girl had to be the friend of the Goddess herself, Alfa Kaoru Nagase.

Though both sisters had been inside Brancott at one point, they'd slipped through their fingers after being driven away by other people's greed and, frankly, stupid decisions. Just thinking about it, she had to have traveled through half the peninsula to reach Balmore, which meant she'd passed through Brancott on her way there. There was even a good chance that she'd have settled down there. In fact, the members of the Hunter's Guild in Baron Renie's territory had said that the girl was planning to do so at one point. If the incident at the restaurant she worked at in the capital hadn't come to pass, she might have stayed there for good. It was something those on the Brancott side would regret for the rest of their days—and the same went for the other countries on the continent, as well.

Balmore wasn't only the production location for the miraculous healing potions, but its development as a country had exploded in recent years. The other countries wanted the girl responsible for spurring that growth, the one who created the potions and who was said to have the same powers as the Goddess Celestine herself—but they wouldn't dare try and do anything rash. Aligot had experienced a crushing defeat doing just that, while the once-influential leaders of Rueda had fallen from power. Not to mention the words Goddess Celestine had spoken that day:

"If you see anyone else doing something bad, just do whatever's necessary to take care of it."

Who knew what sort of punishment constituted "whatever" by a goddess's standards...? But one thing was for sure: no one wanted to find out for themselves. They *were* hoping, however, to invite the girl over at least once for some advice on what to do to further develop their own country.

As for Balmore...

While they may have been a step behind Aligot when it came to shipbuilding, they were still putting up a good fight. They'd already built smaller prototype versions of ships for traversing the open sea, and were currently working on the construction of their first large-scale version of the same type of ship.

They'd also begun introducing crop rotation and the use of fertilizer as part of their farming techniques. It was just about time for the first cycle of crops to be finished from the test fields, and the results were more than clear enough to officially incorporate this strategy into their agricultural practices.

As well, Fearsome Fran and the other four grim reapers who had served as Roland's personal guard—the group who'd protected the country together—were all hailed as heroes. Roland included, they were a group of six warriors who'd caused more than 40,000 of the Aligot Empire's troops to flee in fear. There was no one who could hope to stand a chance against the five knights who'd received the blessing of a goddess, though the four former royal guards had made sure to return the swords they had been granted back to Kaoru. It wasn't like they were true vibroblades or anything, just normal swords that happened to be extra sharp and much sturdier (though they were definitely on another level than your average blade).

Roland's sword, on the other hand, *did* have the high-frequency vibration function, so Kaoru actually had to make sure to *take* the sword back from him. She wasn't planning on letting anyone but her einherjar Francette have one like that. It looked like he had no intention of giving it back to Kaoru on his own, so she had it stashed it away using her Item Box's storage function.

Roland didn't take it well. There was plenty of complaining on his part after Kaoru had confiscated the sword, something along the lines of, "Why was I the only one who didn't get a sword?! It's not fair!"

Kaoru was forced to explain how a royal receiving a sacred sword was actually an incredibly big deal, and it wouldn't only cause Balmore's relations with other countries to get worse, plus it might even make King Serge seem less relevant. Roland finally seemed to settle down after she told him there was a good possibility people would start calling for *him* to take the throne instead. Even after the lecture, he immediately assigned the four royal guards who had received sacred blades to work under him as his personal guard, alongside Francette.

Did he really want a sword that badly?

It was the first time she'd seen the usually calm and collected Roland throw a tantrum like that. A grin crossed her face, as if it actually came as a bit of a relief that she knew even someone like him could act like this, as well.

Kaoru had quit her job at the Maillart Workshop after the peace talks wrapped up. After everything that happened, she had much more on her plate to deal with now, which made it harder to work at a small workshop like theirs. Tears in their eyes, everyone begged her not to go, but her hands were tied.

She had already prepared a replacement, however: Lolotte, an eleven-year-old (when she had taken over) who happened to be a member of the Eyes of the Goddess. She'd always looked after the other children in the group, and had a certain "motherly" personality to her. Kaoru assumed she would be the perfect girl to take care of the five adult-sized "children" at the workshop, and it turned out her intuition was right on the money.

The "cuisine" back when the kids lived in the rundown house had been downright awful, because they'd lacked the proper ingredients and seasonings to make anything decent for themselves. Now that Lolotte had proper cookware and everything she would ever need, she had plenty of chances to let her cooking skills shine. Cooking duties for the Eyes of the Goddess had been handed down to Lucy, another girl from the group who Lolotte had trained up herself. All the girls who had been small and frail due to malnutrition back then had grown up to be lovely young women, as well.

Then there was Emile, the leader of the Eyes of the Goddess. He and Belle, the girl who had thrown herself into the well before, were getting along quite well these days. There was only a four year gap between them, so he wasn't a lolicon or anything.

News of the battle at the well had spread across the country, and figures made in her image were placed near wells after she had become known for protecting them from any evil. She became so popular that offers to adopt her started coming in from all over, and some good ones at that. But Belle had refused them all, choosing to stay with everyone else instead. She never talked about why she'd done that, though. Kaoru could only offer a wry smile, knowing that the girl who had worked so hard to throw poison into the well instead became known as a *protector* of them.

Cedric, the eldest son of the Lyodart household, had gotten married. His fiancée was the aristocratic girl Kaoru had spoken to back during the courting ceremony. Kaoru was overjoyed to hear that, and would come over to visit her every once in a while. She acted much sweeter now, when compared to their first meeting.

Achille seemed to have given up on Kaoru, and now had his sights set on Lolotte instead, which had earned him Kaoru's great displeasure: *"Are you fine with any girl as long as they can cook for you?!"*

Business was booming for the Abili Trade Company. The potion trade was still doing great, of course, but the other new products Kaoru had suggested were a huge hit, as well. This was due to her reputation practically guaranteeing they would sell.

Now that everything had finally calmed down somewhat, Kaoru had realized something: *I don't have any potential husband material...*

And just like that, Kaoru suddenly found herself panicking...

I'm already halfway through my marriageable years, but I don't have a boyfriend, or even someone I would want to go out with. All right, what single guys do I know right now...

King Serge: Pass!

Achille? Have fun getting along with Lolotte, damn it!

There's Hector, the boy from the Earl's household; you know, the same Earl who Francette used to work for. He was thirteen when I first met him, but he's grown up into a fine young man since then... I'll put him on hold for now.

Allan back in Brancott...but things might get dicey if I married someone from another country now, so I'll pass. The prince over there is pretty annoying, too.

Who else... Is that it...? That's all I got? Even if I played along with the idea of going with Hector, he's an earl's heir, and he's younger than me, too...

Oh crap... Am I screwed?

I was a bit shaken up over the predicament I found myself in. As I absentmindedly staggered through the town in a daze, a middle-aged man suddenly jumped in front of me—a dagger in his hand.

"It's your fault... It's your fault the Holy Land was destroyed. We lost everything! DIIIIIIE!!!"

It all happened so suddenly I didn't have the chance to react. The man rushed forward, his blade finding its mark as it plunged directly into my chest.

Chapter 17:
Spreading the Family Genes

"Huh...?" Kaoru stood in a daze as she stared at the dagger that had pierced her chest...mostly because it didn't hurt at all.

"Huh?" The man found himself with the same dumbfounded reaction as Kaoru after seeing she was unharmed.

"Take this! And this! And this!!!" The assailant attempted to stab her over and over again with his dagger—but nothing was happening. Screams erupted from around them as people realized what was going on. Men grabbed whatever weapons they could get their hands on, running to Kaoru's aid.

Kaoru had finally come to her senses and shoved the man away from her. The moment she touched his body—

BOOM!

A bolt of lightning dropped down from clear blue skies, striking the assailant and causing his body to crumble to the ground.

After a bit of investigation into the assailant, it turned out the man had worked as a bishop back when Rueda still was considered a "Holy Land," to no one's surprise. He had embezzled donations, would do unspeakable things to his female followers while claiming he was giving them "the blessings of the Goddess," and generally got away with doing whatever he wanted. His life of depravity had been turned on its head after Kaoru's intervention, and all his ill-gotten gains were confiscated. He'd made his living scamming people in the Goddess's name, so what did he think would happen if he tried harming her best friend? Apparently, he didn't understand that he'd become an enemy of Celestine herself, and his dreams of regaining his past glory would never come true. But it was useless trying to talk sense into him, especially when he was in a frenzy over losing everything he once had.

Kaoru wasn't entirely bothered by the man who had attacked her. So many people had died and so much had been destroyed because of her, so of course there would be some who hated her guts over that.

But something else was bothering Kaoru...

Why didn't that dagger hurt me?

Kaoru didn't have anything to do with the lightning that hit him, either. It wasn't anything that happened because of the explosives she'd made, but a bona fide bolt from the sky. Kaoru had already cut herself on accident plenty of times while cooking, or scraped herself after taking a fall, so it wasn't like she had a body made out of steel or anything.

Then is this some sort of defensive ability that only activates when I'm in danger of dying? I doubt Celes is keeping an eye on me 24/7... So would that lightning be an automatic counterattack? Kaoru thought to herself. *No, I'm overlooking something here. It was something that stuck out to me, but I still overlooked it...*

That's right... It was a few years back when Celes last descended. The conversation we had right before she went away. What did I say to her back then...?

"*If you wait too long, I'll probably end up dying of old age or some sorta freak accident here...*"

"*There's no way that would happen! You tell the funniest jokes, Kaoru.*"

...Did Celes actually think I was joking with her back there?

A joke... So that means it's something that could never happen...

Never...? So dying from old age or in some sorta accident is just impossible, then? Would this automatic defense system just kick in and make it so I wouldn't get killed, no matter what came my way?

Hold on... Then what's going on with my lifespan? Like, I know Celes is a bit ditzy, but she's not an idiot. She was also *especially* aggressive when it came to getting closer with the god of Earth.

There was a huge gap between Celes's sense of time and a normal human's. Even though several months had passed between my first coming to this world and Celes coming down in person, she treated it like only seconds had separated the two events. She talked about things that had happened centuries ago like they were just the other day, after all. Would Celes just let me die after just a few decades when I was the reason she finally had a reason to talk with the god of Earth? Wouldn't she want to stretch that out as much as she could?

Come on, think! What did I ask Celes for when deciding what I wanted for my new body? If I remember correctly...

"Your body will be the same genetically, and back to how you were at fifteen years old."

Fifteen years old...

Fifteen years old...

Fifteen years old...

The body I had...when I was 15...

...She didn't say anything about me growing any more past that, huh.

CELEEEEEES!!!

She got me... She got me good... She totally did that on purpose, I just know it! Even if she hadn't messed with my body, I could've made a potion to make myself younger if I wanted to. Being able to do things like that was the whole reason I decided to go with my potion cheat powers. Was it that she just didn't realize it? Or did she think I would try and die a natural death by just letting myself grow older?

Now I know that I most likely won't be growing any more than this height-wise—and boobs-wise. I could make a potion to force myself to grow up, but I wasn't really a fan of that idea. It kinda felt the same as using platform shoes and stuffing my bra with pads or something. My height would only change a single centimeter, anyway. Japanese people were just short and baby-faced by nature, so a centimeter wasn't going to make any difference.

"I'm leaving on a journey. Please don't come looking for me."

"WHAAAAAAAAAT?!"

All of Balmore was in an uproar over my sudden announcement.

"B-But why...?" Francette asked, her voice trembling.

"I'll be taking a tour around the country to find myself a husband."

"A-A husband? But aren't you supposed to stay a child forever, since you're a goddess?"

"Huh?"

"Huh...?"

"Huuuh?!"

The shocking truth had come to light. It sounded like they thought I'd stay this way forever, just like Celes. I mean, they weren't wrong, as I just figured that out the other day, but I never thought they'd think I'd stay single forever, as well.

I wasn't as popular with the guys lately, so that probably explained why. It's true I might never be able to get married if people thought of me as an eternal twelve-year-old, but *mentally* I'm twenty-seven years old, and my *physical* body is fifteen. I'm already an adult by this world's standards! I'm perfect marriage material!

Wait, did it not matter if I was 1,000 or 10,000? Like, would anyone who tried to marry me when I looked like a little girl just be treated like a criminal? But, this body really is supposed to be fifteen years old, so…

Gahhh! So my only choice really *was* to go out on this trip! I'll pretend like I'm just a normal girl trying to find myself a husband, but this time I'll make sure to let them know I'm a mature, fifteen-year-old woman who just happens to be a bit on the smaller side. I'll just make up something, like "they didn't feed me much when I was a child," as my excuse for being this tiny, and we should be golden!

I'm gonna get my family's genes out there, damn it!

A few days later, and I'd already finished saying my goodbyes to the Eyes of the Goddess. They were all more than capable of living on their own now. I offered to give them the house, but they told me they'd just watch over it until the day I came back. I gave them a bunch of overpowered potions, just in case, and told them to be sure to keep it a secret from everyone else.

If they ever needed to get in contact with me, I handed them one half of a special "voice crystal" I'd made (with a potion inside the crystal) while I stuck the other one in my Item Box. I'd come rushing back if there were any emergencies, probably using a potion I made into the shape of a T*yota Land Cruiser and filled with pseudo-gasoline, or maybe a helicopter that could be piloted using an N*S controller. I'd leave all the complicated stuff like gyroscopic precession, torque, and the angle for the pitch of the blades to whatever powers Celes gave me! I was sure her race had already figured this stuff out back when humans were still single-celled organisms.

But, thinking about it now, were the potions I made so effective because I had Celes's galaxy brain powers there to help me out? Or was it that whatever I was thinking of was made somewhere else and transported over to me? Hmm… Now I was really curious how this worked…

Me leaving also meant Balmore was going to lose their potion supply, but it was never supposed to be this way in the first place. Having them rely on my potions wouldn't only mean getting in the way of their medical advancements, but it would eliminate the need for people who had a talent for medicine. No matter how much I warned them to try and keep those types of people around, they'd just be blinded by the fact that they could gulp down a potion and fix whatever was troubling them. They wouldn't want to keep investing money into medical research and train people capable of putting it into practice. Just the fact that potions existed would probably cause any would-be medical professionals to lose their drive, as well.

That's why, after I fixed up everything that was ailing people at the moment, I was going to have them take care of things on their own from now on. I'd use my healing powers only when I had to while I was out traveling, so I could try to keep my identity a secret. After all, my plan from the start wasn't to have Balmore have the lion's share of miracles to itself, but to spread them out sparingly to the other countries. These healing potions were supposed to be something only a select few could receive as a reward for living honest and diligent lives, not something everyone could use whenever they wanted.

As for the journey, this would be a two-man trip, just Ed and me. Technically, I guess it would be more like a one-girl, one-horse trip.

I packed all my stuff into my Item Box and headed off to the farm that was taking care of Ed. He was already ten years old, which was probably somewhere between thirty-five and forty-five in human years. Going on a trip like this must be rough on a middle-aged man like him. This was going to be much longer than the journey we'd gone on years ago. *Much* longer. I had potions, though, so I figured things should work out all right.

I wondered if he wasn't going to like leaving his old lady behind... I did plan on coming back every once in a while, though, since I wanted to check in on the kids from the Eyes of the Goddess.

By the time I reached the farm, Ed, his wife, and his three-year-old daughter were all there waiting for me.

"Oh, Kaoru, dear. Thank you for always taking care of my husband."

"Do you have any sugar cubes on you, Kaoru?"

"C'mon, now, don't be rude to Kaoru."

...Are you guys really horses? It felt like you've evolved and become something completely different, I swear... And why in the world were Emile and Belle here with their packs slung over their shoulders?!

"We're coming with you."

Yeah, yeah...

I'd seen that look in their eyes before. They were totally set on coming with me, no matter what. I'd already given up on the fact that I was getting some new traveling partners, and we were just getting ready to set out with Ed's family when I found myself with some more unexpected company...

"We shall come with you as well."

And why are *you* here, Francette, with your things packed on your horse? And the king's brother was right next to her, just friggin' shrugging his shoulders!

Well, it wasn't like I couldn't see why he'd be here though... If his fiancée was going off on a trip, and he didn't know when she'd be back, I can see why he'd want to come along, as well. *But you're supposed to be royalty, man...*

The friend of the Goddess, the king's brother, a feared warrior, and the protector of wells... What the hell kinda party had I ended up with?!

...I'd have to think up a nickname for Emile as well, or else I'd just feel bad for him.

Wait a second... Did that mean I was going on a trip with *two* lovey-dovey couples?!

Aw, HELL no!

I was going on this journey to spread the Nagase family's genes, not to help *you* guys get it on, damn it!

After Kaoru had left on her journey, guys from all around Balmore were beating themselves up at the news.

"Wait, Kaoru went off to find a husband? She actually *wanted* to get married?"

"Are you kidding me?! I would've tried chatting her up more if I knew that!"

"WHYYY?!"

"She was fifteen when we first saw her, so she's nineteen now? Is that as big as she's going to get?!"

But they were already far too late...

Chapter 18:
Pushing Through Brancott

Kaoru and her merry companions were currently on the verge of passing the border between Balmore and Brancott. Borders here weren't as big a deal as they were back on Earth, seeing as countries didn't have the manpower or the funds to watch over the entirety of their vast borders. Hell, if you went off the beaten path, through the forest or over the mountains or something, you could cross over into other countries all you liked.

There weren't many people who actually went with that option, however. Why? Simply because they could still get in normally without doing so.

There were no passports or photo IDs in this world. Everything was on paper, so making forgeries was a cinch. You could just swipe a person's documents and pass them off as yours to the guards, no sweat. It wasn't like they had any way of telling if you were the real deal or just faking it.

Border checkpoints were only that in name alone. In reality, they were just small guardhouses, whose main function was to collect a fee from any wagons that passed by them, in accordance with how much they were carrying. Wagons couldn't pass through forests or mountains, so their only choice was to stick to the main roads. Anyone on horseback or foot didn't have to pay the fees for things they brought across since, if they had, smaller merchants wouldn't be able to afford taking their wares across. More evil business practices would run rampant, if that were the case.

Kaoru and her group were on horseback, and had barely any luggage between them. Kaoru had already thrown the heavier and more annoying bits of her stuff inside her Item Box, anyway. Basically, they had a free pass to get across the border.

...Or, that's how it should have been, at least.

"Right this way, please."

As Kaoru and the others tried crossing the border, they were abruptly stopped by a soldier and led to a small guardhouse.

"You must be the angel and her companions? We shall prepare a carriage to guide you to the capital posthaste, so please wait here and relax in the meantime."

How did it end up this way?! Kaoru screamed on the inside.

Before leaving Grua, Kaoru had made sure to say goodbye to her friends and everyone else who had helped her, as well as everyone else who would be affected by her leaving. If she hadn't, who knew what sort of uproar the capital would have been left in. Before they could do anything to stop her or beg her, teary-eyed, for her to stay, she'd already left on her journey.

If they weren't going to take a boat, then the only way to reach the mainland was through Brancott. However, there was a certain "thing" lurking in Brancott: Fernand, the crown prince.

Kaoru wanted to push her way through Brancott before word of her journey got there, since things could get really annoying really fast if they were to get held up there.

With that in mind, she wanted to make it through Brancott as fast as possible, before word traveled to the aristocracy or the royal family. It was all but guaranteed that Fernand would have assigned a spy to keep track of her whereabouts.

When that spy caught wind of Kaoru's journey, instead of using messengers on horseback, they didn't hesitate to send a message through the channels normally used for national emergencies.

The royal palace was in an uproar over the news, of course. Kaoru, the personal friend of the Goddess, was coming to Brancott, and they couldn't let this chance go to waste.

There was absolutely no chance that she could be heading in the opposite direction. The only things to be found there were steep mountain ranges, and further beyond that, the Aligot Empire. If she were setting out on a trip from Balmore, then she had to be heading toward the mainland and, to get there, she'd have to pass through Brancott. Thus, the royal court, aristocrats, and of course, the prince, were all champing at the bit to make the most of this opportunity. They'd placed carriages and elite guards all along the roads into the kingdom, so as to secure her the moment she entered the country.

Oh boy, this doesn't look good. Now what...?

If they haul me off to the palace, they'll start questioning me and asking for all sorts of things. Since this is that arrogant, selfish prince we're talking about, it was totally possible he'd my former co-workers at the restaurant as hostages, just so he can make demands of me. That, or they might be suspicious that I'm actually the same "Kaoru," and try to expose me for who I really am...

Oh crap, oh crap, oh crap!

But this is just a border guard. If I try to make a break for it, then of course he'll send people after me. If they then caught us, they could charge us with illegally crossing the border, and who knows what they'd do to us after that...

Hrmmm...

"Should we off him, Kaoru?" Emile put in, casually suggesting murder.

I'd told Emile to only refer to me as casually as possible right before we left on this trip. It would only attract attention to us if a sixteen-year-old like him was acting incredibly respectful toward me, especially when I only looked to be around twelve.

Belle had just turned twelve and was already a little bit bigger than me. Like her height, and her...ch-chest... All right, sorry! I was trying to make it seem less terrible for me! It wasn't just a little, but a *whole lot* bigger...

We were all pretending Belle was older than I was, and had made her practice being more casual around me, as well. After all those years together, it was a force of habit of hers to keep calling me her big sister, after all. But, considering the situation, it wouldn't be that bad to have me be the older one here, since it wouldn't be all that strange for me to be this small if I was just a year or two older than her. If the gap between us was going to keep on getting bigger, though, then it'd eventually get suspicious. That's why I thought it'd be a better idea to have her be the older one from the beginning... But I guess now wasn't the time to be thinking about all that, huh.

"No offing anyone. I'll try to think of something, so keep cool for now."

"...Got it."

After being led into the guardhouse and offered a seat, the guard brought out wooden cups filled with wine for everyone. Usually a dinky little guardhouse like this should only have some room-temp water, at best, so they probably had this prepared beforehand, on the chance that I happened to come this way. I didn't want to let it go to waste, so I made sure to at least take a sip.

Yeah, that's lukewarm red wine all right...

"Room temperature" was probably more accurate. If anyone in Japan proudly served you a glass of room-temperature wine, though, it'd be pretty hard to be happy about it, and the same went for here.

Their "room temperature" was actually pretty dang warm, but as they didn't really have a way to keep it chilled, I wasn't going to complain.

"So...what seems to be the problem?"

"Oh, no problems here. I received orders from the king to give you a warm welcome, should you enter our kingdom, and to have you escorted to the royal palace immediately," the man explained. It appeared he was no ordinary guard, but a slightly higher-ranking soldier, posted here to lead me to the palace.

"What makes you think I'm Kaoru?"

"All the higher-ranking soldiers of our country were present to see you during the proceedings in Balmore and committed your appearance to memory. Our regular soldiers merely memorized what you look like after studying your portraits."

Gyahhh!!! What the hell is that about?! So you're not gonna just let me go, is that it?! Just how tenacious are you, man?! Are you a stalker or something?!

I was planning on playing dumb, but it looked like he was certain I was the Kaoru they were looking for. He was probably going to argue back if I denied it now, so my only choice was to give up and admit it. If I tried denying it and things got heated, my "big brother" Roland, his fiancée Francette, and my other "brother" Emile might try slicing and dicing their way out of this—*especially* Francette. Things could get dicey real fast...literally.

By the way, here was our current story: Roland was the oldest son of the family and engaged to Francette, while Emile was the second-oldest and Belle was *his* fiancée. I was the oldest daughter of our makeshift family, of course.

I could have made us all brothers and sisters, but that would have been plain weird to have the two couples flirting with each other when they were supposed to be related by blood. I didn't want any weird rumors floating around about us, so that was why I went with the current setup instead. I wanted to avoid *any* stories of brother and sister complexes among our group, thank you very much.

Still, no matter how you sliced it, Roland looked like royalty, while Emile looked like the most common commoner you'd ever laid your eyes on. I was planning on explaining it away by saying that Emile was an illegitimate child, conceived with a maid and raised like a commoner, but I was pretty sure it wouldn't come up. It'd take a fairly reckless person to pry into a noble's family affairs.

Anyway, our reason for traveling was that Roland wanted to take a trip to another country while he was still young, and his brother-from-another-mother Emile was there to accompany him, as well as their two fiancées. I was here as the chaperone to watch over the two couples.

Based on my smooth skin and the other decidedly not-commoner-like features about me, I was planning on saying I was the sheltered daughter of some lower-ranking aristocrat who was not at all wise to the ways of the world. That would also make it seem more natural for everyone to prioritize protecting me without raising any suspicions.

…What, you think that's pushing it? Look, don't worry about it. This is the kind of situation where they'd probably expect a more believable lie if we wanted to fool them, and that'll actually make our story even more credible! Sheesh, get off my back…

Oh yeah, I wasn't calling Roland "sir" or anything on this trip, either. I know he's the brother of a king, but he was the one who had decided to tag along with me. I was just going to treat him like another one of my traveling companions. It'd be a pain in the butt to give him special treatment when everyone else was supposed to

163

be acting more casual around each other. If we kept calling him "sir" all the time, people were bound to find out that something was up eventually, though I made sure to ask him if it was all right first.

…Not like he could really say no to me, though.

"We've finished preparing a carriage for you, so if you will just follow me this way…"

The guard made to lead us somewhere, but I casually brushed him off.

"Oh, no thanks. Ed and the others would get jealous if we rode something being pulled by other horses!"

"Huh…?"

"I guess we'll be off, now!" I stood up from my seat, and the other four followed suit.

"W-Wait! Hold on a second, please!"

We ignored the panicking soldier as we left the guardhouse. We hopped on our horses once we were outside and set off once more. We'd already made sure to talk things over, with me declining his offer to be taken anywhere by carriage. Now they shouldn't be able to say we tried to illegally force our way across the border.

Consequently, the checkpoint was in complete chaos as we left it behind us.

"I wonder if that guy sent a messenger on ahead?" I yelled to Roland over the sound of galloping horses.

"Yeah, I bet they already took off a while ago!"

"Then how about we give them the slip?"

"Let's do it!"

I figured that the soldier from before would come chasing after us, with the carriage he had prepared for me in tow. But that would never be able to catch up with us, so it didn't really matter. We'd make it to the capital ahead of the messenger, finish what we needed to do, and get out of there before they could do anything about it. For

CHAPTER 18: PUSHING THROUGH BRANCOTT

that to happen, though, we'd need about a twelve-hour head start. If we could just make it through the capital and speed along faster than their messenger horses, then no one would be able to keep up with us. Not only did we have Ed's family, but we also had horses specially bred to be used by royalty. I even had healing potions. No problems there.

"Hi ho, Silver!" I shouted, trying to set the mood a little.

Ed got mad at me.

"You're using that name again! Just what kind of horse are you cheating on me with, missy?!"

…Sorry.

It didn't take long for us to overtake someone we assumed to be a messenger, but we were expecting that. It was going to take them a good few days to reach the capital, so they had to keep to a certain pace to get there at all. They couldn't just keep pushing their horse as hard as they could, or else they'd just run it into the ground. It was possible they could've prepared other replacement horses and switched them out every few hours or so, but that probably wasn't the case. They didn't know where I was coming from in the first place, and they also thought I'd be slowly trundling along in the carriage they'd prepared for me.

The messenger stared at us in blank amazement as we passed him by. If he tried chasing after us now, his horse definitely wasn't going to make it without collapsing at some point. Thinking about it from his side, he might have been in shock that we appeared to be so reckless as to push our horses this hard. No matter what happened, I doubted a common soldier would have enough cash on him to buy replacement horses that he hadn't planned on getting in the first place. All he could do was focus on trying to reach the capital as fast as he could within his available means. He was most likely thinking that we couldn't possibly keep up this pace, either, and that he'd be passing our exhausted horses in no time. He didn't once think this gap between us would keep getting wider as we got closer to the capital...

It had gotten dark, so we started getting ready to set up camp. All I had to do was take out our tent, which was already put together, from my Item Box, and it was ready in an instant. We were traveling light, since we had only packed the essentials, and we could keep pushing on until it was too dark to press onward, since it took no time for us to get our camp gear ready. The messenger, on the other hand, would have to stop at a town to take care of his horse and rest for the night, which meant the distance between us was only going to get greater.

Horses needed substantial water and care, so pushing them to the brink and then leaving them outside to set up camp was highly impractical—if you didn't have cheat powers, that is. At this rate, keeping our twelve-hour lead would be a piece of cake, and I wanted to put that time to use when we were in the capital.

At first, I was just planning on being as stealthy as possible while getting into Aras, so I hadn't really been concerned with a time limit. I'd sneak in, then sneak back out. Easy. But now that we were racing against the messenger before he could tell the country I'd arrived, my plans had changed to charging through as fast as possible.

Ed and the others were practically jumping for joy at all the feed, apples, corn, sugar cubes, and potions I gave them, but then I received this comment:

"Excuse me, Kaoru? Could you not give my daughter so many sugar cubes, hm?"

Now Ed's old mare was getting mad at me...

Leaving the messenger in our dust long ago, we finally arrived in Aras, the capital of Brancott.

There were plenty of people who knew me from back when I lived and worked here as a waitress, but even if we ran into them, it still wouldn't be a problem.

If we ran into someone who knew that I'm the Goddess's friend, though, then I'd really be in trouble. There were people who had happened to catch a glimpse of me during the peace talks in Balmore and, according to that border guard, there were plenty of other soldiers who'd been ordered to memorize the details of my appearance. That was why I had decided to go ahead and change my hair and eye color again, and have everyone walk all around me, so I wouldn't stand out as much. Despite that, no one in my party so much as batted an eye at my sudden transformation. To them, I wasn't the "friend of the Goddess" everyone else knew me as, but rather a goddess from another world entirely.

There was only one place I really wanted to visit in the capital. After hitching Ed and the other horses up, I used another potion to change my hair and eye color before opening up the doors.

"Hey everyone, long time no see!"

"K-Kaoru!!!"

That's right, I was back at the Big Belly Bistro, the restaurant I had once worked at as a waitress, where I had run my own counseling service.

"K-K-Kaoru!" The landlord came running out of the kitchen after hearing everyone call my name, throwing her arms around me and squeezing tight.

I-I can't breathe!

"You were okay after all! We were all so worried about you when we heard you disappeared! People said you'd been hurt! It must've been so hard for you...and you haven't grown even a little bit since then..."

Oof... Hitting me right where it hurts...

"Kaoru!"

The next person to come running over and give me a big hug was Aimee.

...You're still working here? Shouldn't it be about time for you to move on, girl?

"Thank goodness... Thank goodness!" she cried repeatedly, tears of joy streaming down her face.

"H-Hey, where's Agathe?"

"She went off and got married to one of our merchant regulars!" Aimee pouted. "He only had a tiny business at first, but the moment he married Agathe, it suddenly took off. Now her new father-in-law calls her 'the gift of the Goddess.' She even has two beautiful baby boys! She couldn't get any happier if she tried, tch!"

Ah... I know how you feel, Aimee! I know that feeling so much it hurts!

As I stewed in my feelings of simultaneous empathy and jealousy, the door to the restaurant suddenly flew open.

"Kaoru!"

Speak of the devil. Agathe came running inside, tears welling up in her eyes. One of the customers had apparently had the good sense to let her know that I was here. It looked like her new family basically lived next door.

She might be a mother of two now, but she'll always be the cute little Agathe I waitressed with. That said, she *was* a married woman, so I almost felt like I should be adding a "Mrs." in front of her name or something.

"Kaoru, I heard about your injuries! Are you all fixed now?!"

"Oh, yeah. I got to take a swig of this amazing medicine, 'the tears of the goddess,' and that patched me up, good as new."

"Th-Thank goodness... I tried putting all the things you told us about into practice at my husband's company after I got married! When I did, we got a huge surge of customers, and our business really took off! Even now, the trade guild still calls me things like 'the ideal wife for a businessman,' and I have all this influence at the gatherings of the merchants' wives, and... Oh, you know what, never mind."

Yeah, I kinda figured that's what happened. Agathe and Aimee had overheard the advice I gave customers when I ran my consultation service, and I made sure to tell them the essentials of the Japanese service industry on our breaks and stuff. They both should have had an even playing field, since they both learned the same things from me, but I wonder how Aimee and Agathe's situations had ended up so different? It was truly a mystery...

Afterward, I introduced Roland and the others to my former co-workers as my traveling companions. I then proceeded to have a great time chatting with the restaurant staff and the regular customers.

Fran had left to find us an inn sometime during all the talking, so that meant I had a free pass to smashed-ville, population *me*.

...Or that's what I thought, but they wouldn't let me have alcohol, and said that kids drinking booze "was a bad thing." I already looked like this four and a half years ago, people! I was way over fifteen now, which meant I was absolutely a proper adult!

Everyone pretended to be surprised, but they just handed me juice anyway.

Damn it... Really, guys?

Roland and the others sipped at their tea and said that they weren't foolish enough to drink alcohol smack-dab in the center of enemy territory.

Oh yeah, I guess this is *"enemy territory" for them...*

After that, we all had a good time reminiscing about the good old days. It was a ton of fun for me, but eventually it had to come to an end, as all good things do. Not getting home at a decent hour for most of them would just start up all kinds of family issues.

Should you really be here instead of with your new family, Agathe? Well, I suppose she is *the head of her family, so she's probably fine...*

I made sure to ask everyone a favor as the festivities wrapped up.

"Hey, all, can I ask you to do something for me? I don't want you to refer to me as the Kaoru from four and a half years ago, but as her older sister, who just happened to stop by and see the restaurant that had been so kind to her younger sibling. Otherwise, those people who chased me away in the first place are just going to catch on and come after me..."

Everyone agreed, of course. Even if one of them messed up and let it slip, the others would step in and play it off by saying something like, "What, you couldn't tell the difference? I know they look alike, but weren't you listening to what she said?"

Someone suggested that I call myself the *younger* sister, since my appearance hadn't changed at all from the last time I was here, but I'd already told the prince before that the older one was living here in Aras.

Crap... I messed up on that one.

When I woke up, I found myself in one of the capital's inns. I hadn't actually gotten around to drinking last night, but I was pretty wiped from all the partying we did.

It had been a long time since I'd had a good night's sleep in a proper bed. After we figured out our sleeping arrangements for the night, Fran took Ed and the other horses to the stables to make sure they were taken care of. They must have picked up on what she was trying to do and as a result they just followed after her. Not gonna lie, that was pretty dang convenient. I was sure it must have been a little shocking to anyone who saw Fran leading that train of five horses without her actually doing anything...

I was the last one up, apparently, since everyone had already washed their faces and gotten dressed.

C'mon, at least wake me up, guys!

And why was everyone all gathered around me and staring at me while I was asleep?!

You all like to ogle a girl's face while she's sleeping, is that it?!

Anyway, whatever. We usually slept all huddled together when we were camping, so they'd already seen what I looked like when I was asleep... Still didn't mean that I liked what was going on here, though.

I ain't putting on a show, people! I'm gonna start charging if you wanna look that bad!

...The scary part was, I feel like they'd actually have been happy to pay for that show.

After finishing up breakfast, we were on our way again. Nothing seemed out of the ordinary around the inn, so it looked like the messenger still hadn't arrived yet. I suppose that even professional messengers must have to turn in for the night. Traveling by starlight wasn't just exhausting, it was also inefficient. Getting a good night's sleep and getting yourself ready for the next day was far and away the more efficient choice, which meant that we shouldn't have lost any of our lead, and the gap between us should still be about the same. That meant that we didn't really have to force ourselves to go faster than we already were.

Considering the composition of our group and that I had potions to hand out, we were leagues faster than a single messenger who didn't have any replacement horses to get him to the capital efficiently. After we got out of this country, we could camp outside less and begin spending the night at inns more often. We could even stick around in each location a bit longer to give this a more "road trip" feel to our journey.

Dang, I'm starting to get excited about this! All right, time to get out of here!

"Well done on spotting Miss Kaoru! I'll be sure to reward those guards at the border for their efforts. When should we be expecting her arrival?"

It was evening when, in the audience chamber of the royal palace, the king and his son, Crown Prince Fernand, were all smiles after hearing the news. The messenger who had brought it, though, didn't seem quite as ecstatic.

"I'm not so sure about that, Your Majesty..."

"Hm? They're using one of the carriages we had stationed all around the border, no? So I'm sure you must be able to at least make an estimate, depending on when they set off, correct?"

"W-Well...it appears Miss Kaoru and her group didn't use the carriage we prepared, and instead chose to continue on using their own horses..." the messenger answered hesitantly.

"Well now! They may have preferred their own trusty steeds over a carriage, I suppose. There are those who put their own horses over any others, after all, so I suppose there's nothing to be done about that... Then, what time should we expect them to arrive?"

"They passed by me fairly quickly after I first set off, and I haven't seen them since, Your Majesty..."

"Wh-What was that?!"

"They shouldn't have been able to keep that pace up all the way to the capital. Their horses would have collapsed from exhaustion in no time at all. That's why I assume they must have either strayed from the main road to take their rest, or otherwise they pushed their horses too far and now their journey is at a standstill. Since I don't know which scenario they're in right now, it's a little difficult to predict when they will arrive..."

"Ah-ha, I see. So that's what you meant." The king looked relieved to hear that and sat himself back down, after having been on the edge of his seat just moments before.

Fernand, on the other hand, looked anything but at ease.

"Did you consider that Kaoru is almost certainly carrying healing potions?" he said, barging into the conversation.

"Oh..."

The king and the messenger were at a loss for words. Over the past four years or so, the so-called "Miss Kaoru researchers" of the capital had come to the conclusion that she had some sort of invisible bag that could be filled with any number of potions that she might need. There were plenty of situations where it wouldn't make sense otherwise—particularly the war against the Aligot Empire—and there were even those who'd seen Kaoru pull things out of thin air.

Normally, there wouldn't be anyone who would even think of using valuable healing potions on their horses, but this was Kaoru, after all. The word "normal" didn't really apply to her.

"Gather all the soldiers you can! I want them scouring the capital for Miss Kaoru, and the rest of them stationed on all the roads coming into and out of Aras, now! Fernand, you head to that restaurant, just to be safe!"

Everyone who was gathered in the room scattered and rushed out in a hurry, with Fernand not even offering a reply to his father before dashing out of the audience chamber himself.

"Yeah, we had Kaoru's big sister stop by here last night. So what?"

"Wh-What?!"

The owner of the restaurant answered brusquely, since he recognized Fernand as that "Fernie" guy who'd hounded Kaoru when she still worked as a waitress. Kaoru had given instructions in case something like this was to happen, and they made sure to follow them and give him the runaround. Still, there was one detail that didn't escape Fernand:

If Kaoru and her sister had supposedly not met since they had gone their separate ways, then there was no way that she would know about the restaurant.

That had to have been Kaoru herself...

"But, boy, were we surprised to get a customer out of the blue who looked just like Kaoru! Some of our workers even went over and started hugging her! It really turned into quite the commotion, I tell ya."

"Huh?"

"After everything settled down and we heard her out, that's when we figured out she was Kaoru's sister. Even she was surprised!

She had no idea the restaurant that she'd happened to pass by was where her little sister used to work. We all decided to throw her a welcome party last night, and it got a little crazy, what with all the celebrating we did."

"…"

Right when he thought he had solid proof, it had gone up in smoke in an instant. If only Fernand had been there when it had happened, then he would have known… No matter how much he regretted it now, there was no changing the fact that he hadn't been, though.

"Did the sister say anything about what she was planning on doing next?"

The owner thought things over for a second before acting like she had just remembered something.

"She didn't say where she was going, but she was absolutely livid when she heard Kaoru had been hurt and chased out of the capital. Can't say I blame her. She kept muttering things like, 'They tricked her,' and, 'I'll never forgive them,' with this terrifying look on her face. Her eyes were scary enough to make kids cry, I tell you! Just like her little sister."

Fernand turned pale as soon as he heard those words. He had a horrible feeling that he knew who the "they" and "them" Kaoru's sister had been referring to were…

A horrible, chilling feeling…

"S-So, where is Kaoru…I-I mean, Kaoru's big sister, now?" Fernand asked, his voice trembling slightly.

"Who knows? I think the people traveling with her must have found an inn somewhere."

The moment he heard that, Fernand left the restaurant without offering a word of thanks.

175

"Tch. You may be hiding the fact you're a prince, but to me, you're nothing but a scumbag. Like hell I'm gonna forgive the person responsible for driving Kaoru away in the first place!" the owner spat out, after the prince had left.

Kaoru had figured Fernand would come sniffing around to try and find her, and it looked like her prediction was right on the money.

Fernand made a beeline for the first inn he could find. While most people would have thought it was obvious to search the inns first, the prince was only searching the more luxurious inns, the ones that the nobility and important merchants might stay at.

It *was* true that at least half of Kaoru's traveling companions were used to staying in such grand places. They *did* have a king's brother, his fiancée (who happened to be a national hero in her own right), and a goddess with them, after all. But Kaoru would never stay at any of those inns, and she'd made sure to tell everyone as much immediately after setting off on this trip. Francette would never have chosen one of those fancy places to spend the night.

All this went to show how little Fernand truly knew about Kaoru, and that all his work was nothing more than wasted effort...

"So she left early this morning then?"

"Yes, Your Majesty!"

The search of the capital was still ongoing. According to the soldiers who had been sent to investigate the inns, however, it appeared that Kaoru and the others had left the capital first thing in the morning. All they'd discovered was that she'd cleared out of her room, but it was apparent that they weren't planning on staying longer if they'd already packed up all their things and left. There was also a possibility that they hadn't liked the inn they had stayed at and had moved on to find another one, but that was a slim chance at best, especially since the guards had already done a sweep of every inn in the capital.

"What about stationing troops along the roads to follow her?!"

"We've already sent word to them, Your Majesty, but it was already evening by the time we received your orders. We called an emergency assembly and split our forces into squads after giving them their mission, but trying to travel on a moonless night would only have brought harm to the horses. That's why it was decided that they are to set out first thing tomorrow morning."

"Hrm… We'll be a whole day behind her, but I suppose there's nothing we can do about that…"

The king of Brancott wasn't ready to give up just yet. Kaoru's group had pushed themselves to the brink just to reach the capital before the messenger, but now that they'd achieved their goal, they wouldn't have to move as fast anymore… That was his reasoning, at least.

But having returned after searching the inns, Fernand had a hunch about just what was going to happen… He had the awful, sneaking suspicion that she was going to slip through their fingers yet again.

"So this is the town you wanted to visit, Kaoru?"

"Yup! I only really want to poke my head in and say hi to the guild, so I doubt it'll take that long."

It looked like Francette had finally gotten used to acting casual around me (even though it took Belle and Emile almost no time at all). Her body might be younger, but it looked like the inside of her head was just as empty as ever… Though, I shouldn't really be talking smack about her, since I could practically feel some karma creeping up, ready to smack me right back for that.

All right, time to go inside!

It was way earlier in the day now than the first time I'd come to the guild. If I had decided not to visit during the busier hours, then only the people on the night shift would have been here, which meant I'd have even less of a chance of seeing who I came here for. That was why I aimed for peak business hours, when most of the employees for the guild would have to be on duty.

Jingle, jingle.

All eyes were on me when they heard the bell above the door announce me coming in. Yup, just the same as last time. The only thing different now was that, instead of going back to whatever they were doing before, they kept on staring at me.

...It was a pretty big difference, actually.

"Huh? I-Is that you, Little Miss Angel?"

Hey, it's the guy who gave me some sausage back then! After he asked me for that massage, I was flooded with all sorts of requests that got me food and copper coins. I'll never forget what you did for me, man!

"Thank goodness you're all right!"

And the boar steak guy, too!

"Gene!" the scary-looking receptionist who'd taken care of me when I first got here shouted. With a silent nod, the hunter whose name she called stood up and latched the front door shut, with the other hunters getting to work shutting the windows as well.

Uhhh... What's going on here?

Roland and Fran put their hands on the hilts of their swords, while Emile and Belle stood on either side of me. Emile had his hand on his sword as well, but Belle was still hiding that she was carrying a knife. The tension in the air was so thick that you could cut it with said knife, which was when the receptionist shouted out for all to hear:

"We're so glad to have you back at our humble guild, Miss Kaoru, friend of the Goddess. On behalf of the guild, let me offer you our most heartfelt greetings to have you here. This time, we swear to the Goddess Celestine that we won't let you be taken away by any rotten, fat-cat aristocrat!"

She came out from behind her counter and knelt down before me. Now that the other hunters knew who I was, they followed suit as well.

Roland and the others finally breathed a sigh of relief and took their hands from their swords. That included Belle, whose hand had been twitching in anticipation, waiting to pull out her knife at a moment's notice.

Back when I first began selling my potions, my lack of stock and not having proper distribution channels meant that they only circulated domestically. When they finally began spreading outside the country, I made sure that this was the first town they were shipped out to, and that the people here received priority shipments of potions appropriate for how much a small town in the sticks with its own guild would use. I was sure that those who were distributing the potions were confused as to why some tiny, far-flung town in the middle of nowhere was getting that much before the royal capital even got any, but they weren't about to question the creator of the miracle medicine—and for good reason, too.

As soon as the potions arrived at the guild, the staff knew exactly what the items were—and who had made them. Afterward, the members heard one piece of shocking news after the other: the war with Aligot; the descent of the Goddess at the peace talks; Aligot's miraculous comeback after the war; the end of the Holy Land of Rueda... And at the center of all this was a single girl.

Even though they hadn't been able to protect the girl from being taken away, she was still trying to show how thankful she was for what they had done for her in her time of need. They'd been waiting for the day she might return to this town, just so they could show their gratitude to her—or that's what I wanted to think, at least.

But I didn't want people kneeling before me. I wasn't into that sort of thing. That was why I took a different approach...

"I'm starving! Does anyone want a massage? I'd be willing to take two sausages or a quarter of a boar steak as payment!"

Everyone stared at me blankly for a moment before they caught on to what I was trying to say.

"If it's sausages ya want, leave 'em to me! I'm gettin' 'em, and I ain't lettin' anyone say otherwise!"

"Then I guess I got that boar steak covered. Right... Now who's the guy who got the drink before?"

"That was Dalson, right? He's out on a job right now, so I'll cover for him!"

"Damn, does he have some bad timing! I bet he's gonna be kicking himself when he hears about this..."

Laughter broke out among the guild members as they stood up, and I got to work tending to their massaging needs.

"M-Miss Kaoru, what are you doing?! Please, stop!"

Francette went back to being all formal in her rush to try and stop me, but I just ignored her. This was the first town I'd visited, where I got my start in this world. Everything had begun right here.

Before I knew it, I felt my mouth twitching. Yup, this was my smile, all right... I get told to stop showing it so much, since it makes kids cry, though.

When I glanced up, I could see the scary receptionist lady's lips curled back to reveal her teeth as she made some sort of horrifying expression... Oh, wait, I guess that was a smile, too, huh?

"Me next!"

"Then me after him!"

With a swift elbow strike from Fran and a pinch on the back of his hand from Belle, Roland and Emile's cheerful remarks quickly turned into yelps of pain.

Time flies when you're having fun, and this was no exception.

"Right, then it's about time for me to get going."

"I see... Feel free to come stop by again anytime," Gilda, the receptionist, said, back to her normal self now.

The other hunters were there to see me off as well, and... *Oh yeah, that's right!*

"Scary recep— Er, Gilda...take this."

Oh crap, I can't believe I almost forgot!

I pulled a small wooden box from out of my Item Box.

"What's this?" she asked, a curious expression on her face.

"Do you understand what I mean when I say that I'm leaving the country?"

She thought things over for a second before the realization set in. "Th-There won't be any more potions going around?"

Ding ding ding, we have a winner!

"These are specially made potions with Celes's blessing. Their quality will never deteriorate; in other words, they have no expiration date."

Everyone's breath, hunters and workers alike, caught in their throats when they heard just what I'd given her.

"I-If anyone found out about these..."

It was only natural for her to be worried, and her concern was certainly not unfounded. It was all but guaranteed that the nobles would come to take them for themselves. But I'd already planned ahead for just that possibility!

"Not to worry, they'll lose any effects they have the moment they leave this building. Also, if anyone other than a pure, worthy person belonging to this guild tries to use the potions for themselves, then they'll turn into poison."

Despite calling it poison, it'd only give them about two or three days of cramps and nausea. They'd definitely wish they were dead by the end of it, though.

Of course, everyone at the guild turned pale from shock when they heard my explanation, and rightfully so.

"That's why I think everything should be alright. So, with that, good luck, everyone."

Gilda made like she was going to kneel again, but I stopped her by throwing my arms around her instead.

Oh, no, you don't! I hate it when people do stuff like that!

"Huh…?" Gilda was taken aback by the sudden hug.

"I hate it when people do that," I said softly to her.

"You do, huh… I guess you would, wouldn't you?" Gilda said with a grin.

"Hehe…"

"Ahaha…"

We shared a laugh and smiled at each other. Two very horrific, unsettling smiles, at that.

"Oh, Goddess, what am I looking at?!"

"They look like they're the heads of some sinister organization or something!"

"I'm gonna have nightmares about this tonight…"

"Shut it!"

After Kaoru and the others had gone, the people gathered there ended up kneeling once more. It looked like it was going to take some more time before the closed-off guild was back to normal.

Chapter 19:
A Brave New World

Our five horses continued on through the dark of night, a small, flickering blue light leading their way. I couldn't shake the feeling that one of the baron's lackeys would come for me if we stayed in that town, so we ended up leaving in the middle of the night. I wasn't planning on having us keep pushing on until morning, though. We'd go just far enough to get out of the baron's territory, then make camp in the forest or something, as long as it was off the main road. That way, the baron wouldn't have any authority. He didn't stand a chance if he wanted to try and take me away by force, anyway.

We had the brave and honorable brother of a king; the hero who had saved her country and wielded a legendary blade; two fanatics willing to throw their lives away if it meant protecting the Goddess; a legendary sword and knife between them all—and a goddess herself. Even if the baron mustered all the troops he had available, they wouldn't last even a few minutes.

The light we were following was that chemical you could find in glow sticks and stuff, just with the brightness turned up to eleven. I added a reflective plate to that and, voila, now we could light the way in front of us.

We weren't really in a rush to get anywhere, so it was plenty bright enough to get us to the next town at a leisurely pace. I tried using a gas lamp (or, more accurately, a carbide lamp) to try and keep with the feel of the world, but gave up when Ed showed some, uh, "slight," resistance to the idea.

"Yeowch! That's hot, missy! What do you think you're doing back there?!"

The horses all bristled at me for trying to use the gas lamps, so there wasn't much I could do about that.

All you had to do was fill a container with calcium carbide and water to make a gas lamp, and if you stuck a valve on it to control how much gas was released from the chemical reaction inside, you'd have yourself a simple, compact, and long-lasting light source. I thought it was the perfect time to use them, but it seemed Ed and the others thought I was just horsing around...

Heh. Horse puns.

Maybe it was because I didn't go for a traditional lamp with the cover on it, but instead the ones used for fishing that had the flame exposed... Personally, I had my own idea of what those lamps looked like in my head: a long pole with a sturdy rubber band attached to one end, a lamp on the other, strolling about in the river at night and trying to see what you could fish up. I know they had banned them in most places back in Japan, but this is a whole different world.

All right, I'm totally gonna try doing that at a river sometime! Maybe the next time we make camp by one or something.

I still thought they were the best when it came to spelunking or fishing, but considering that I had the power to create potion containers with whatever features I wanted them to have, it didn't really matter if it was a glow stick or a lamp or whatever. I wasn't about to try and force my tastes on anyone.

After finally making it out of the baron's territory, we kept on moving forward for about an hour, until we picked a random spot to veer off the main road and set up camp. Everyone was nice and full now, so, after we all downed healing potions, we made sure to get Ed and the other horses all taken care of. I scattered some of my homemade bug repellant about, pulled out my bed from my Item Box, and hopped onto it with Belle to catch some sleep.

This bed had really come in handy over the years, I tell ya... Oh yeah, and just to make this clear, I make sure to air out the mattress and sheets in the sunlight, and to wash and change the sheets, too. Now that I think about it, this was the first time in five years that this bed had finally gotten to pay a visit back home!

We may be running away in the opposite direction this time, but I've been looking forward to sleeping on you forever and ever, good ol' bed o' mine.

As for Fran and the boys, they were already curled up on the grass. I made sure to give them some blankets from my Item Box, which I'm sure was more than plenty for warriors like them, since they were used to roughing it on the battlefield.

A few days later and we had made it across Brancott's borders without incident. We were now in Drisard, a country to the northeast that shared a border with Brancott. There weren't any border checks here, but there were supposed to be some once we reached the first town.

It was a heavily fortified city with walls surrounding it on all sides. It wasn't like they were on bad terms with Brancott or anything, but it *was* another country's territory, and so our first stop was the Walled City of Selinas, a place that housed a decent amount of soldiers and acted as a stopping point for trade and business.

Drisard was the first country we had reached after a long stretch of roughing it outdoors, so I wanted to stay in the city for a good few days and study up on what Drisard was like. It's said that whoever controls information controls the world, after all. Roland and the

CHAPTER 19: A BRAVE NEW WORLD

others may have been knowledgeable about the four countries that surrounded Balmore, but not so much for anything outside that range. That was to be expected, really. Even if they had taken the time to learn about the political affairs of other countries, it wasn't like they could have gone in person themselves, so they wouldn't have had much of a chance to get any kind of fresh info. The same went for the other countries, as well.

Roland was fairly well-known in his own country and the ones surrounding it, but here, he was the brother of the king of some country that didn't really have anything to do with them. People might know the names of the royal family, the higher ranking nobles, or certain military officials, but anyone else might as well be a nobody to them. The name of the protector of the Goddess still hadn't quite reached that far, and, in fact, the name "Fearsome Fran" was more famous than the other title I'd given her.

But considering how young Francette looked now, there wouldn't be anyone who would think she was the same "Fearsome Fran" from the war against Aligot all those years ago. Not to mention, Francette is a pretty common name, too, sorry to say.

The same went for me, as well. Considering how long ago this happened and how old I looked now, my appearance definitely wouldn't match up to the rumors about me, though the countries surrounding Balmore should already know that much.

I had plenty of different variations in what people called me, too. Just like how Celestine's name was also known as "Celestines" or "Celestia" and all sorts of other variations, I was also known as "Carol," "Kaol," "Demon Eyes," "Executioner," and a whole bunch of other nicknames. It was exactly like what happened when you played the "Telephone Game" with people.

187

...But what's with those last two?!

There were also a ton of girls who had been given my name over the past four years. It was almost blasphemous to name your child after a goddess, but it was no problem if a goddess had taken on a human name because she liked the sound of it. There were plenty of people out there who were hoping to gain even the tiniest sliver of favor from the Goddess, which explained the name's sudden spike in popularity. That was why Kaoru, Carol, Kaol, and all those other names that sounded similar had suddenly become commonplace in this world (though it didn't seem like there were any parents who wanted to name their kids "Demon Eyes" or "Executioner"). That people called me an "angel" and a "messenger of the Goddess" was actually pretty well-known as well, but not enough that those nicknames became proper nouns or anything.

Anyways, what I've been trying to get at after that paragraphs-long explanation is that we wouldn't need to make fake names for ourselves from here on out. The word may have already spread that I'd left Balmore, but it probably wasn't the same for the king's brother and Fearsome Fran being with me, as well. Roland had been trying to stay out of the limelight in the first place, in order to support his brother, King Serge, and it wasn't like Balmore wanted to let everyone know that their most powerful warrior wasn't home.

If you think about it, we probably stood out much less as a bunch of aristocratic siblings (plus some extras) on a pleasure trip, rather than people on the journey for the sake of a twelve-year-old girl, which was better for hiding my true identity. Three of us carrying swords wouldn't be strange at all, considering we had no entourage of guards to protect us, and that included the fact that two of them looked decidedly knightly.

Right, looks like I'm giving the goddess-slash-angel thing a rest for the time being. I wasn't the czar of the roaring potion trade in Balmore anymore, but the sheltered daughter of some lower-class aristocratic family, on a journey to study what it was like out in the real world. I'd be taking this opportunity to make some money while I was at it, too. I'd already made a killing selling my potions before, but it never hurt to have more money, especially when you just happened to have an Item Box with infinite space inside of it. If I ever ended up with money to spare, it might even be a good idea to start investing in Aligot's shipping industry, or maybe even start up my own shipping company.

Oh, yeah... Back when I was a kid, I always thought that "czar" was Russian for "bizarre" and they just shortened it, like it was slang or something. It was only around middle school that I found out what it really meant, not realizing that it wouldn't make sense in the first place, since they probably had a different word to say "bizarre."

Gahhh, I feel like such an idiot whenever I remember that... I don't even want to think about it... But anyway! It's time to put my cringy past behind me and start a brand new adventure!

Eventually, we spotted something that looked like walls far off in the distance.

So that must be the Walled City of Selinas!

This was the third country I'd visited since reincarnating in this world, and the first town of that country was waiting just ahead of us. (Though I technically haven't been reborn, I do have a completely different body, and Celes did make me younger. This is more a reincarnation than just being transported to another world. Just saying.)

Alrighty, let's get out there and do this!

We'd finally arrived at the Walled City of Selinas. It was a surprisingly simple task getting inside: All we had to do was get in line, then say where we came from and why we came to Selinas. It wasn't like they had the facilities to do a thorough background check here, and they couldn't spare the time to conduct one, either. They just checked the wagons for taxable items and took any obviously suspicious people to the guardhouse to compare them to the wanted posters they had on hand. With Roland giving off the aura of an elite, Francette looking like a knight, me looking like some kind of aristocrat's daughter, and Emile and Belle looking like our escorts, there was basically no chance of them stopping us.

"We're from the household of Earl Adan in the Kingdom of Balmore. I'm traveling together with my siblings to other countries in the pursuit of knowledge."

That's all it took from Roland to get us through. There wasn't any guard who'd dare meddle with an aristocrat from another country. We'd obtained permission from the earl himself to use his name, should anyone pry, so there shouldn't be any problems there. Not that there was ever a chance of that happening, though.

Even then, while we said we were with the Adan household, that didn't necessarily mean we were Earl Adan's kids or anything. If we were just employed there, we could still technically say we were "with" them. So long as we at least acted the part, it wouldn't be a problem.

I didn't want to lie, so I made sure to get one copper coin from the earl before heading out as an advance payment for all the stories I'd tell him when I got back. Since he had paid me to do so, that meant I could proudly state I was officially employed by the Adan family. Done and done.

"Woohoo! Our first town in a brand new country!"

The people who heard me shout smiled as they looked our way. Roland and Francette's smiles, however, were more on the wry side after hearing me get so worked up.

Lighten up! Putting your feelings into words just makes you appreciate it all the more! I look like a twelve-year-old girl anyways, so there's no problem with me getting a little excited, damn it!

First things first, we needed to find ourselves an inn. We'd be in trouble if we put that off and ended up not having a place to stay. We couldn't really go for any hoity-toity places, but it'd also be strange for us to go somewhere that was too cheap when a majority of our group were girls.

Right, let's try and find someplace somewhere in the middle of the fanciness scale, then.

After asking a bored-looking lady for recommendations, I finally settled on an inn after watching the people coming in and out of it.

"Excuse me, do you have any rooms? We need two doubles and one single."

Like hell I'm gonna get stuck in a room with one of these lovey-dovey couples!

"Yup, you got it!" the lady behind the counter answered. After running her eyes across us, she had a look of pity when she stopped at me.

...I don't need your sympathy, lady!

The sun was still high up in the sky. We could find something to eat and gather information after it got dark, so I was going to take this time to do some sightseeing around town.

Roland and Fran were sharing one room, while Emile and Belle were in the other. I knew they were young and all, but we all huddled together to sleep when we were out camping anyways, and Emile and Belle had known each other since they were kids, so I couldn't just tell them what to do now. With them all in their rooms, I snuck out to take a look at the town.

...It's not much different here from the towns in Balmore.

I mean, I knew this wasn't some country on the other side of the ocean or anything, and it wasn't like crossing some invisible border would suddenly cause the weather and plant life to change out of nowhere. The people's dialects and mannerisms were pretty much the same, too.

Even border lines would change slightly over the years, though it'd definitely take some time before that happened. I'd have to travel a little farther if I wanted to get that elusive "exotic country" feeling.

I walked through the town, checking out the market stalls and their prices before coming across a slightly more rundown street. As I walked along it, I suddenly found myself with two men standing in my way. Turning around, I saw another two had blocked off the path behind me. These weren't some sneering street thugs, but men who actually looked like they meant business.

Yeah, it doesn't look like this happened by chance... They were totally aiming for me. Well, crap. What do I do now...?

...And that was how I ended up in a cell. There was nothing I could really do about it, especially with my twigs for arms. Even if I tried to resist, they would've just pinned me down and made me regret it. My automatic defenses might have kicked in if they tried to stab me, but so what? Even if they didn't, I couldn't really resist if they had me held down, anyway. Having them twist my arms or getting punched would still hurt, you know?

I'd had some pretty painful experiences here, falling down or getting my fingers caught in doors and stuff, but Celes's automatic defense system hadn't activated then. Also, if I was wrong and that defense mechanism didn't activate every time, then what? What if it turned out that Celes just so happened to be looking by some random chance when that crazy guy with the knife came at me last time? I was too damn scared to try risking my life just to see if that was true or not!

I was pretty sure the people who had captured me didn't really want to kill me, though, which was why I let myself get taken without putting up much of a fight. They wouldn't be able to get any money out of me if I was dead, after all. There were plenty of chances for me to escape, so I wasn't too worried about it. But that was where the real problem came in...

"*Sniff...* It hurts..."

"I want to go home..."

It wasn't just me who had been captured. It looked like they hadn't gone after me because they knew who I was; so why then? These people probably saw me as a twelve-year-old girl who belonged to the family of a wealthy trader or some aristocrat. Since I was staying at the inn, that meant I was either on my way to Brancott, or I'd just come in from Brancott and was on my way to Drisard. That also meant I shouldn't have any connections in this town, so even if the people I came with did try looking for me, they'd have trouble finding their way around. If they could escape with me over the border, then there wasn't anything anyone could really do.

My conclusion: They were just your average kidnapping ring. I mean, there were only girls here, and cute ones at that. If they only went after the prettiest girls, I couldn't be *too* hard on them, since that must be the reason why they went after me. Yup, definitely that.

But it's not like I'm happy over being kidnapped just because they think I'm cute. Seriously, I'm not!

"What's wrong?"

Back at the inn, Roland and Francette had left their room to meet up with everyone for dinner. It was then they'd found Emile and Belle standing outside the door to Kaoru's room.

"Well...no matter how much we knock, Miss—I mean, Kaoru, won't answer..." Emile said, hastily correcting what he called Kaoru. Even if it looked like there was no one around, you could never be too careful.

"She's either sound asleep, has gone to the bathroom, or is already on the first floor eating... I say we head downstairs for now," Roland said, heading for the staircase. They couldn't just break down the door to check, so the other three reluctantly followed after him.

"Have you seen the girl who came with us?" Roland asked the lady running the front desk on the first floor.

"Oh, the little raven-haired girl? She left as soon as she got her room."

"WHAT?!"

Not only did Kaoru like to eat, she was quite the stickler when it came to money, as well. There was no way she would pass up on dinner after paying for it along with her room.

Even if she had gone out for a stroll, she'd have been back by the time evening came around. That was just the type of girl she was, and everyone knew that well. If she wasn't back by now, that meant that she was in trouble.

"We're leaving!"

Roland slammed his key down on the counter, followed immediately after by Emile. They only had those two keys between the two groups, so the girls ran right out of the inn after them.

What to do, what to do...

It seemed they'd brought me to a secret room inside one of the rundown houses in a poorer district. A corner of the room had been sectioned off and made into a cage where they were holding me and three other girls. The others looked to be anywhere from five to ten years old.

...I know I'm over twenty, but I don't wanna hear any snide remarks about that!

By the way, I'd dedicated the day I arrived in this world as my "fifteenth birthday." I make sure to celebrate it every year...by myself. People would ask how old I was if I invited them, so I kept my birthday a secret.

Putting that aside for now, I should probably figure out what to do about this. While this place was a bit on the small side, it was split into two separate rooms. At the bottom of the stairs was a room with a fairly large table, about five or six chairs, a shelf, and several wooden boxes spread out everywhere. Half of the room we were in was this holding cell made up of a lattice of sturdy wooden bars, while the other half had a small table and a single chair. Beside me and the group of kidnapped girls, the only other person in this room was a guy acting as a lookout. He was currently spacing out in a chair outside our cell.

Before I could start thinking about what to do next...

"Ow... *Sniff...*"

It looked like they'd been pretty rough with the five- or six-year-old when they'd captured her, as she was holding her left shoulder in pain. She was practically a kid. I couldn't just ignore a cute girl in pain! Oh, but that didn't mean I thought it was okay to ignore girls who weren't cute! I'm serious here, come on!

195

Anyway...

"Eek!"

I slipped a hand into the collar of the girl's shirt and began rubbing her shoulder...while creating a healing potion in the palm of my hand. I placed my other free hand on top of her clothes and made a flicking motion toward the guy sitting outside the cell.

"Pain, pain, go away!"

"Agh!" The man let out a scream of pain.

"Go away!"

"Ow?!"

"Go awaaay!"

"ARGHHH?!" The man jumped up from his chair, face flushed, and screamed at me. "Wh-What the hell did you just do?!"

Hehe, looks like that surprised him. I only sprinkled a bit of potion on his body that caused an excruciating amount of pain, is all.

"Who, me? I didn't do anything, honest. This girl looks like she's in pain, so I thought I'd say a little magic charm to try and take her mind off it. See, just like this: Pain, pain, go away!"

"GAH?! S-Stop that! If you don't, then..." The man gripped the hilt of his sword.

"There's also one called 'sword, sword, go away' as well," I said, a smile on my face. "That one makes anyone who tries brandishing a sword have it thrust back into them instead...painfully."

"A-Ahhhhhh!"

Oh, he ran away...

"It doesn't hurt anymore..."

The girl looked up at me blankly before breaking out into a big smile.

Yup, I'd say a smile is one of the best looks a girl can wear.

"What's going on in here?!" the apparent leader of the kidnappers shouted as he burst into the room. He wasn't one of the four people who had nabbed me; it looked like he'd been waiting here on standby instead. He was in his early thirties, and actually looked to be a relatively normal person.

Well, that's not too strange, I figured. I'd heard only the underlings for yakuza and other gangs tried to act tough and pick fights, but the higher-ranking members actually looked pretty normal. Outside of work, they generally acted like ordinary people, as well. It wasn't like they were going to go around staring daggers at their wife's or daughter's friends, even if they were gangsters. They just happened to have a bit of a harsher look in their eyes... Actually, let's just stop talking about people with harsh looks in their eyes. It's not like I'm one to talk.

...*Damn it.*

The leader guy was the only one to come into the room. The lookout from before was probably too scared to come back, I imagined.

"Huh? Nothing's going on, really. The man sitting there was sleeping when he suddenly jumped up and ran out of the room."

I balled up my hands and brought them in front of my mouth as I said that. It was the most cutesy, innocent, childlike pose I could think of, and I'd always wanted to try doing it at least once—when no one I knew was around, of course. I didn't even want to think of how much they'd make fun of me if they ever saw this. Probably that it "totally doesn't suit me" or "it's creeping me out" or something.

...*Shut up, me!*

"That damn idiot, sleeping on the job..." the leader angrily muttered to himself before heading back into the other room.

Yup, that's the way. You guys go on and start fighting in the other room.

"Is anyone else hurt?"

The two other girls, besides the one I still had in my arms, shook their heads.

"You don't have to worry about a thing. Help will be here soon enough."

"It will...?" a girl around ten years old looked up to me and asked.

"Yup. All we have to do is sit back and wait. Hey, do you wanna play a game? The rules are super easy, so you should be able to get them right away!"

It'd be pretty easy to call for help if I really felt like it. If I made another huge explosion like I had during the war with Aligot, or created a pillar of golden clouds, Roland and Francette should catch on right away. But it was still a little early to be resorting to those. The main culprits hadn't shown their faces yet, after all: the ringleaders, the ones pulling the strings and controlling the group that was kidnapping all these cute girls. (Note that I'm absolutely remembering to keep the word "cute" in there.)

I'd imagine this group wasn't just made up of these five guys. They might be the ones actually carrying out the kidnappings, but I figured they wouldn't be enough to handle transporting the kidnapped girls, finding a buyer to sell them to, or getting hold of people to help smuggle them out of Selinas. No matter if you were a merchant, someone in power, or an evil organization, you had to have someone backing you from behind the scenes. That was just the standard for how these things played out, no doubt about it!

"Wh-What the hell do you think you're doing?!" the man who ran into the cell screamed when he saw us playing games. It wasn't the leader or the lookout from before, but a different guy this time.

Then there was us, playing a game of Reversi, that game that was pretty similar to Othello. I'd made the board, and the black and white pieces, myself.

"This? I've had it the whole time, actually," I said, pointing toward the leather bag on the floor.

"Huh?" the man's eyes were wide open as he stared at the bag in a daze.

A few moments passed…

"You… You did?"

"You bet I did."

The man didn't look too satisfied with my answer as he sat himself down back in his chair. I even went through the trouble of making the board so obviously big that it clearly wouldn't have been able to fit in my bag, yet he didn't notice at all.

Wow… Are you for real right now?

Then, a little while later…

"…What in the world are you eating?"

"Well, as you can see, we've got some bread, extra-large meat skewers, and grape juice."

"Where did you get that from?!"

"From this bag…"

"LIKE HELL THAT'D ALL FIT IN THERE!!!"

The four of us in the cage were all holding bread and huge meat skewers in both hands, with big cups of grape juice by our feet. There was no way that would have all fit into the tiny bag I had—not normally, anyway.

"It fits just fine. Everyone, put your skewers and cups in here when you're done, okay?"

"All right!"

Four sets of cups and skewers were thus put away into the impossibly small bag.

"Th-That ain't right! There's no way that can all fit in there!" the man screamed, running out of the room with bloodshot eyes, just like the first guy had done.

I bet he's going to go call the leader again...

He was the only one with the key, and the lookouts couldn't open the cell themselves. It was a pretty good way of dealing with stupid lookouts who could get tricked easily, or who thought about laying their grubby hands on the goods. They did need to go to the leader every time if anything happened, though.

"Again with this crap?! What is it this time?!"

The leader and the lookout from before came back together.

"Th-These guys have some kinda freaky bag in there..."

"Where?"

"U-Uh..."

We were all that was inside the cell, of course. There was no bag, no juice—nothing.

" ... "

"Are you being serious?! Are you all just screwing with me?!" the leader bellowed.

He wasn't referring to us, of course, but the second guy who'd been on lookout duty.

"Do you all just go calling for me whenever you have a bad dream, is that it?! More than that, why the hell are you sleeping on the job in the first place?! They may be kids, but what the hell do you think it means to be on lookout, huh?!"

It was like he was disciplining a new employee or something. I wondered if he was going to make the guy go scream in front of people about how worthless he was at this job... Oof, I didn't even wanna think about it.

But putting that aside...

"Hey, girls. You got any games or meat skewers in there?"

The four of us shook our heads.

...*Uh-oh, looks like the eight-year-old has some sauce on her cheeks from the skewers...*

"You. Come with me."

The leader took the lookout by the ear and dragged him into the other room. It seemed they hadn't noticed the sauce, luckily enough.

"All right, girls, I'm gonna explain what our next plan is while they're gone!"

"Okay!"

"...Sheesh, the hell was that all about..." the third lookout muttered to himself as he came into the room. He was some guy who looked like he was in his early twenties. "My shift wasn't supposed to be until tomorrow... I should've just gone out drinking when I had the chance, dammit."

"Um, what happened to the other people?"

"They're getting an earful from the boss right now. They've all gotta be idiots for making that much of a fuss over a few bad dreams, I'm telling ya."

Huh, this guy was much friendlier than the other two. Maybe he liked talking, or maybe he just liked kids...though I didn't think he'd be doing this work if it was the latter. I mean, it was true that he could just happen to be doing this on the side to make ends meet or something.

Regardless, I can't let this chance to get some info go to waste!

"Um… What's going to happen to us now?" I asked, making sure my voice was as uneasy-sounding as possible. I did that same cutesy pose as earlier, too, for good measure. If I didn't do it now, I didn't know when I'd get the chance to do it again, so I made sure to do it as much as I could!

"W-Well, let's see… No one's gonna hurt you anymore, and your life isn't in any danger, so you don't have to worry about any of that. You'll never have to worry about going hungry, and you might even get to live a pretty good life, too. I mean, you might end up having to do, like, maid work or something, but they won't be making you do heavy labor or anything. If you get them to take care of you, you might get to live your life as if you were, I dunno, the fourth-born daughter in a lower-class noble family or something. Man, I'm getting jealous…"

Yeah, considering his line of work would get him hanged if he was caught, I bet he really would envy that kinda life.

He said that like he meant it from the very bottom of his heart. But what he was describing was pretty much, you know…being a slave. A sex slave, by the sound of it. Pretty much as bad a crime as it gets. Kidnapping us was a crime, of course, but outside of judicial slavery, all other forms of enslavement were illegal in this country, whether that was buying, selling, or using slaves.

"Judicial slavery" might have the word "slavery" in it, but it's actually one of the sentences you could receive after being convicted of a crime. There aren't any countries in this world charitable enough to feed criminals for free, so even lesser crimes could earn you the death penalty. That's still a bit too cruel even for them, though, and a waste of potential human resources as well. That's why those on death row were either sent to work as laborers in the mines, or as shock troopers in times of war. Prisoners-turned-shock-troopers were able to get their sentences reduced the longer they stayed alive and the better they performed in battle, so it was better than the fate the mine laborers faced, as they would just slowly waste away until death took them.

Aside from that, the perpetrators could be sentenced to slavery for life, or for however long their sentence was otherwise. But the fact of the matter was that only criminals could be slaves. Any children born to slaves weren't actually guilty of anything, so they could live their lives as relatively normal citizens. It was just that their parents were criminals, that was all. If they committed any sort of crime while still a minor, a thorough investigation was conducted to determine whether their parents or another adult had forced them to do it, or if it was something they'd had to do to survive.

In short, unless there was some sort of extenuating circumstance, having little girl slaves who were less than ten years old wasn't only illegal, but a serious felony. Selling, owning, whatever—everyone who was involved in the process was guilty of the same crime. That was why even the slightest leak could spell the end for all of them, and if anyone reported them, it could lead to the whole group being wiped out. They wouldn't be able to pull any of this off if they didn't have someone backing them from the shadows.

"Where are we being taken after this?" I asked in a quivering voice.

The lookout must have figured there was no harm telling us, since we wouldn't be able to do anything about it, because he answered without so much as a second thought.

"To the estates of some of the local nobles or some well-to-do merchants. The capital is way too risky to even think about, and most of the more powerful aristocrats and big merchants wouldn't dare take the chance. They can already use their own money or authority to get any young girl they have their eye on, you know. That's why you're all going to some less-important aristocrats, or maybe one of the smaller merchants from around here. If I'm being honest, they're people out in the sticks who can't go out and nab a girl for themselves, since people would realize something was up."

"Oh..."

Yep, I read you loud and clear.

So basically, it meant the four of us might all be going to different places. If that was the case, I had to finish this before I left town...

"Does that mean we have to stay here until then?"

"Actually, it looks like we'll be getting out of here by the time morning comes around."

I didn't know if he was bored, just liked talking, or liked keeping little girls company. He was probably a lolico— I mean, a nice guy who just wanted to calm some scared little girls down. Probably. And since they were about to whisk us away, without any further chance to talk with anyone outside this cell, he probably thought it was fine to tell me at least that much. We'd figure it out once we arrived where we were going, anyway.

"The boss was saying that we were supposed to wait until we had one or two more, but it looks like someone out there is really tearing up the town trying to find you. Not to mention, the last two guys seem kind of emotionally unstable now, so we're going to cut it off with just you guys this time."

Good, all according to keikaku!

Oh, "keikaku" means "plan," by the way.

I tried getting some sleep, since they were probably going to come wake us up early the next morning, but the guard ended up talking to me so much that I couldn't really get any shut-eye. After asking so many questions, it was only polite on my part to hear him out. That was why I humored him, at least, but it didn't seem like he was going to stop anytime soon…

…*Wait, he's on the night shift, so he's not going to sleep in the first place! Like hell I'm gonna put up with this all night!*

He finally let me go after I told him it'd be rough traveling by cart without getting some sleep. And the other three, you ask? They were fast asleep the whole time, while leaving me to talk with the lookout!

Right around daybreak the next day, I woke up after hearing a noise. When I turned to get a better look, I saw the leader and his four men had come into the room. Looked like it was time to get going.

The leader opened the cell, and the other kidnappers came to tie us up one at a time before shoving pieces of cloth in our mouths to gag us. They were being incredibly thorough about this.

They kept our legs unbound and walked us up the staircase before leading us outside. Of course, I didn't forget to leave them a little present with my potion-making ability, once we made it to the top of the stairs…

When we left the rundown shack they'd been keeping us in, I could see the silhouette of a wagon coming into view. They forced us into the back, which was when they finally bound our feet.

There were six empty barrels stacked in there, and…you wanna bet on what happened next? C'mon, I'd be willing to bet you a gold coin on it. Though I figure none of you would place such an obvious bet…

With two empty barrels and four more filled with cute girls, the wagon took off toward the city gates.

As soon as they put the lid on the barrels, I pulled a knife out of my Item Box. This position was really uncomfortable, so I cut through the bindings around my ankles first, then through the ones on my wrists. I thought about making something that would melt through the rope, but I didn't want to end up melting my own body as well, so I went with a knife instead. Even if I nicked myself a little, I'd be fine if I drank a healing potion after.

It was a simple matter cutting through the rope, especially when I made a potion container I shaped like a vibroknife to do it. It even slashed straight through my hands—and boy did it slash them good.

YEOWWWWWW!!!

P-Potion! Potion, now!!!

It was only after I drank the potion I realized something: I could have just stored the rope in my Item Box without cutting it.

Arghhhhhh!!! Why am I such an idiot?! All that pain, and all for friggin' nothing! Gah, I need to take this grudge out on someone, now!

After some time had passed, the cart stopped. I could hear voices coming from outside.

"What cargo do you have in there?"

"We're carrying six empty casks, and we're on our way to fill them with wine."

"Then I'll go and confirm... Hm... Yup, that's six casks, all right... You're clear to proceed!"

Seriously? You're not gonna check if they're actually empty?! Oh, whatever—now's my chance!

I busted through the lid of the barrel I'd cut up with my knife before, popping out of the top and yelling at the top of my lungs:

"These guys are kidnapping little girls! Please, help us!"

"Yup, those are certainly *empty* casks. Go on through!"

"Thank you kindly."

"Huh…?"

The guard who'd lifted the flap of the wagon's tarp was staring right at me, a sneer on his face. He stood alongside someone who looked like a merchant and one of the wagon's guards, both of whom I'd never seen before. The merchant and the escort climbed into the wagon, getting ready to tie me up again.

Oh, I get it… So they're all in cahoots with each other…

I'd already unraveled how most of their operation worked, so I was done playing along, not to mention that I was kinda pissed off at this point, too.

All right, let's do this!

I created several gourd-shaped potion containers right above the wagon, the same ones from the war with Aligot. You know, the ones that were filled with pseudo-nitroglycerin and concentrated sulfuric acid.

The sound of a thunderous explosion rocked the area. I created a pillar of golden clouds spiraling skyward as a marker to let Roland and Francette know where I was. To top it all off…

"A pinch of sunlight."

I reached out and made like I was grabbing a ray of sunshine that was peeking through the tarp of the wagon, hiding the fact that I had just created a miniature spray can in my hand. You gotta do these things in style when you're putting on a show, ya feel me?

As for the contents of the can, well…

The men who attempted to climb into the wagon to subdue me had frozen in place because of the explosions and my strange movements. I turned toward them and shouted:

"Have a taste of my special technique! *Breath of the Goddess!*"

"AAAAAAGH!!!"

While I yelled the name of something that sounded more like a spell than a special technique, I blasted them with my freshly-made pepper spray. That didn't mean that the Goddess's breath was so rank it could incapacitate someone, though. Who knew what Celes would do if that rumor started going around...

...I should probably change the name of my special move.

As the other guards and members in the wagon came rushing over to see what the commotion was about, I had a faceful of pepper spray waiting for them for their trouble. Since the guards hadn't come rushing to my aid when I was yelling earlier, it was safe to assume they were all in on the kidnapping operation, as well. Even if some of them happened to be innocent, it wasn't like the spray had any lingering effects, and I always had healing potions if it came down to it, too.

All I had to do now was wait for the soldiers to show up, and... Oh, yeah, I had to let everyone out of the barrels. It wasn't like I forgot about them or anything... I just didn't want them to get taken hostage, or for them to breathe in the pepper spray, or, you know...

Okay, I forgot! I'm sorry!

Just to be safe, I made another spray that could knock a person out cold with one shot and made sure to use it on everyone writhing around on the ground.

Maybe I should have just made that from the beginning...

Well, I guess they did need to learn their lesson, so the pepper spray didn't go to waste after all! That was the reason I was sticking with.

After ten minutes or so had passed, the line of hunters and merchants waiting to get out of town had begun to grow restless when they realized they weren't moving at all. It was right around then that the silhouettes of four people came rushing out from the center of town. They gradually came closer and closer, until...

"Oh, Fran!"

As the one with the most stamina, Fran was leading the group, followed by Roland, then Emile and Belle, who were way behind but bringing up the rear nonetheless.

"Don't you 'oh, Fran' me!"

Oh dear, she doesn't seem too happy with me...

I should keep my mouth shut for the time being.

"Do you know how worried we were?! We spent the whole night running around town looking for you... What were you doing this whole time?!"

Fran was usually so respectful when talking with me, but this was the first time I'd seen her this furious. I decided to come clean and give her an honest answer, since it was almost guaranteed things would get ugly if I tried to lie my way out of this now and flubbed it.

So, I shouted as loud as I could for the people around to hear, "Well, I actually ended up being kidnapped by a group who were only going after cute girls. The kidnappers are in the back of the wagon, and these girls are the other victims they've snatched. The guards knocked out around the wagon were conspiring with the kidnappers, too!"

Ow... My throat hurts from all this yelling.

"WHAAAAAAT?!"

Fran, the rest of my group, and everyone who'd gathered around exclaimed in shock. I could understand why they'd be so surprised. If there had been a gang of serial kidnappers in a town as

209

small as this one, you could bet there would have been rumors about it already. If the guards were in on it as well, it was going to be a huge scandal for the governor, once he found out about it.

Kidnapping and illegal slave trafficking—both crimes far and away worse than robbery. Considering its proximity to other countries, there was an extremely high chance that foreign visitors had been victims, as well. At worst, it could even turn into an international incident.

Before long, an enormous mass of people came marching toward us from the center of town.

Yeah, I was thinking it's about time they showed up.

The *real* soldiers of Selinas had arrived.

"What's going on here?!"

A group of a few dozen soldiers finally appeared on the scene, probably arriving from whatever barracks they'd been stationed at. This *was* the city closest to the national border, after all, so of course everyone on duty would come running if there were explosions and strange pillars of golden smoke by the gates. I'd be more surprised if they *didn't* come. I'd imagine those who weren't already here were probably gearing up right this moment.

No matter how good of terms they might be on with their neighboring countries, they wouldn't let their guard down enough so as to not be prepared for an invasion. There was always a chance of a sudden raid, which was why there was an inordinate number of soldiers for a town the size of Selinas. No other towns this far from the border would be able to house this many of them.

"What's going on?! Is there anyone who knows what happened here?!" the commander of the soldiers shouted out, having his men circle the wagon.

Town guards and wagon guards alike were scattered on the ground like leaves, and a group of three armed men and women were standing right next to them. Under normal circumstances, they'd be arrested on the spot, no questions asked. Among those three potential suspects, however, was a man with an appearance that suggested he was anything but an average commoner; a female knight wearing an expensive-looking set of armor; and a young man who looked to be their attendant, likely charged with their protection. Their swords were all sheathed, and they didn't seem particularly panicked over the situation.

Standing beside them was a group of young girls, with Belle (who only *looked* like she wasn't armed) and me probably being counted as part of that group. We didn't look like the type of people who'd try to forcibly push our way through the gate, no matter how you sliced it. The guards were bound to come running if we were to just stay here, so it was unthinkable that we'd just hang around waiting for that to happen. If we wanted to try running back into town, or make a break for it, we would've already hightailed it out of here by now.

This was the commander, the man in charge of dealing with emergency situations, so it was a safe bet that he was no fool. He'd ordered his men to surround us, just in case, but he wasn't going to jump the gun and make a heavy-handed decision without hearing us out first.

"You there. Can *you* explain what happened here?"

The commander had directed the question toward Roland, since he seemed like the most likely one to be in charge here. Roland, however, just turned to look at me instead, seeming hopelessly lost. That was why I was the one to explain what happened in his stead.

Pretty much what always happened, really.

"The owners of this wagon are just a small part of a group of serial kidnappers who target cute girls! The guards laying on the ground knew they were transporting girls they'd abducted, and are in league with the kidnappers!"

No way I'm letting up on using "cute." No matter how painful the incredulous stare Fran sent my way may be, I'm never giving that up.

This might be the last time I'd have the honor of saying I'd been kidnapped by people who only target cute girls, after all. I had to make sure people understood that it wasn't just your ordinary kidnapping ring, but a cute girls kidnapping ring! And though I say it's a "cute girls" kidnapping ring, that didn't mean that the members were cute girls themselves. I'd imagine there were plenty of people out there who'd want to be captured by a group like that...

"Wh-What did you say?!"

The commander recoiled, making a face like he'd just stuck lemon concentrate in his mouth. He must have been aware of the kidnappings, and he was probably happy as an officer of the peace that the culprits had been caught, especially since the guards were the ones who'd catch the blame for the decline in public safety if the criminals stayed on the loose.

However, there was something very inconvenient for him mixed up with my explanation: that the guards were in league with the kidnappers. And not just one of them, but all six who'd been watching the city gates. This was a scandal the likes of which they'd never seen before, and could become a much bigger problem if the top brass caught wind of it. This was essentially the "face" of Drisard, due to it bordering so many countries, after all.

"So...you're saying these three took care of six guards, when two of them look like they're barely of age? And without giving them any time to take any of the girls hostage...?"

"Oh, no, that's not quite right," I responded instantly, before Roland and the others had the chance to make any weird excuses.

They were bound to interview the other witnesses to get the facts straight; not only was this a huge problem in and of itself, but a massive issue for the army, as well. This wasn't going to end with testimony from only one side. Well...so long as *they* weren't working with the kidnappers, too...

"What? Then who could have..."

"The Goddess."

"Huh?"

"Like I said, it was the work of the Goddess. She used her powers to subdue these evil people, then created the rumbling and golden clouds to summon her devout followers. That's who you all happen to be, right? You're all devout followers of the Goddess?"

"H-Hrm... If that was all meant to summon her most devout followers, then I suppose that may have been referring to us..."

He seemed confused, but, at the same time, a little proud to say that. It was easy to see why, since being called to service as a loyal servant of the Goddess was an honor that would follow him for the rest of his life. It was more valuable than any medal he could receive.

"So, um...h-have you met her? The Goddess, that is..."

"Yes, that's right. She's the absolute epitome of beauty, although compared to her statues, her chest is a little...no, *much* smaller...in person."

I wasn't lying. I just didn't mention *when* I'd met with her.

"O-Oh, I see!"

CLANG

"Gah?!"

213

Ow, ow, ow!

A giant wash pan suddenly appeared out of the sky and fell directly onto my head. It looked like Celes had just so happened to be checking in on me right then...

"P-Please, just forget about that last part..."

The commander had gone white. He could only frantically nod back.

I could already feel a lump forming on my poor, aching head...

I know I can fix it with a bit of healing potion, but you really whacked me good, stupid Celes... That thing wasn't made out of aluminum, I'll have you know! It was wood, and wood is friggin' HEAVY! What're you doing stealing old jokes from back on Earth, dang it! I don't know if the God in charge of Earth told you about that, or if you've been sneaking peeks at Earth for yourself, but you can make your boobs whatever size you want! I'm the one who should be feeling sad here, you ass!

Huff, huff...

Well, at least the commander seemed like he believed me completely after that, so I guess it all worked out.

"All right, I guess I'll have you all come with me to headquarters, then."

"No thanks!"

"...Huh?" The commander could only stare blankly back at me after I so casually brushed off his order.

"Those six other soldiers were part of a kidnapping ring targeting cute girls. I don't know how many other soldiers are also working with them, so I'm not just gonna blindly follow you somewhere. I wasn't born yesterday, you know."

The commander fell silent, unable to refute my point. Still, he wasn't just going to let me go that easily.

"N-No, I can't allow that! We have to fulfill our duties as well, you see…"

The commander couldn't pull any funny business with the people who had been saved by the Goddess Celestine herself. That was why he still wore that troubled look on his face, even though he wasn't backing down. It'd be an even bigger pain if they took us to a military building or to see the governor or something.

Hmm, now this is a dilemma. What to do, what to do… Oh, I know! I still have that strategy that's always worked for me before!

"Well, I don't know what people will do to me if I get taken away somewhere private, with no witnesses around, so I'm going to have to refuse. I don't wanna spend too much time here, since I need to hurry and get to the next town. In that case, I'd like you to tell your superiors that I'll answer any questions they have in the waiting area over there. We're leaving just before noon, so if you need us for anything, you should make any requests you might have before then. I'd also like to ask that you contact the families of the girls who were kidnapped. My family is already here, as you can see…" I said, pointing to Roland and the others.

"No, erm, well…"

"But, if none of that's necessary, then we'll just be on our way."

"W-Wait! Please, wait!"

The commander was obviously flustered after seeing I had no intention of giving up.

"I happen to value my life, so I won't back down on any of this. If we just stay here wasting time, that's just less time for you before I leave."

After mentally wrestling over what to do about the situation, the commander eventually ran off...but not before leaving a group of soldiers behind to keep an eye on us. I wasn't planning on tricking him and trying to sneak away or anything...

I mean it!

Oh, maybe he left those soldiers to watch over the kidnappers, since he was in such a rush and didn't have time to deal with them. But they were all looking at us, for some reason.

You should be watching the guys on the ground over there! They're the real criminals here!

Chapter 20:
Spreading the Family Genes... Or Not!

After about an hour of waiting, another group of soldiers appeared from the town. It looked like there was a change of plans after the commander came back to report what had happened, and the soldiers who were gearing up were reassigned to arrive with some important bigwig instead. Now, was it going to be some big shot from the military, or the governor...

We were standing just in front of the town gates, in an entrance meant for wagons. There was a huge crowd of people gathered around us. Rumors were already going around that the Goddess had appeared here, so there wasn't anyone who would take a chance on leaving now. The rumors had spread all the way to the town, as well, and those who had heard them had come in droves to see for themselves.

While we were waiting, Belle and Emile had gone back to the inn to take care of the bill and grab our luggage. They also brought Ed and the other horses back with them, so we were ready to leave at any time.

"Are you the ones who met with the Goddess Celestine?!" a man in his early fifties shouted as he stepped out of the wagon he arrived in. Judging by what he was wearing, he had to be the governor, the exact person I had expected.

Not only had I practically shouted in front of everyone about how the guards were in cahoots with the kidnappers, but there was also talk of the Goddess having appeared here. It'd be more shocking, honestly, if there was a governor who'd actually let someone else handle this situation. At worst, news of the scandal could end up reaching the royal palace or even other countries. However, if he played his cards right, not only could he play down the incident, Selinas could make a name for itself as a site where the Goddess had descended. He wouldn't dare leave something that could decide the future of his household to one of his subordinates.

"Yes, that's right."

I wasn't going to get all ultra-formal with him, even if he was the governor. Roland and Francette would get angry with me if I did and probably say something like, *"No matter how much you may be pretending, I can't allow a goddess to debase herself by conforming to human customs!"*

...Especially Francette, to be frank.

I mean, I *was* pretending to be an aristocrat's daughter right now. There probably wasn't any need to grovel before another noble in the first place, and he probably thought I was only about twelve or thirteen years old, anyway.

"Then explain to me what's happened here!"

Seemed that he didn't care about all the eyes and ears that had gathered around us. Actually, there was probably a better chance that he'd already heard about how the guards were working with the kidnappers, and he was getting ready to cover that up by making sure everyone could hear what he had to say about it. If that was the case, he might actually be one of the more clever governors I'd met.

The reason he might not have already tried hauling us away was probably because he'd heard the talk about the Goddess appearing and believed in it; alternately, he didn't, and was only taking the appropriate action on the off chance that it *might* be the truth.

There wasn't anyone in this world who didn't believe in the Goddess Celestine. She actually did show up from time to time, and there were plenty of big shots from other countries present when she had appeared just four years prior. It'd come as a bit of a shock if there was anyone who thought she didn't exist.

Celes was also known for being pretty severe with her divine punishments, even going so far as to get innocent people caught up whenever she dished out her judgment. There were even stories of her blithely ignoring those in need when they were inside the blast radius. There wasn't anyone in this world who had the guts to tell lies using her name, including criminals.

That was why he'd be an idiot to not believe my story. I was pretty sure he must have heard about the wash pan that fell from the sky, too...

So while he'd probably heard the whole story already, I'd imagine the main reason he'd want to hear what happened directly from me wasn't just to confirm what had gone down, but also to use it as a way to appeal to the people. The crowd was filled with merchants from his own territories and from other fiefdoms, or even from other countries. And not just merchants, of course, but perhaps even spies, as well...

Even if he *did* find out what had happened, I doubted the governor would try to summarily strip us of our status or put everyone involved to death, or anything like that. There wasn't much benefit to doing anything that dangerous, and the governor in charge of an area like this should easily be able to figure out how to handle a cute girl like me.

That was why it was probably a safe bet the governor wasn't connected to the kidnapping ring. In that case, I'd have no problem settling this peacefully.

...So long as he was ready to remove the corruption at the source, that is.

"We're all from the household of Earl Adan, in the Kingdom of Balmore. When I was out about town, I was abducted suddenly and forced into a cell in the basement of one of the houses here. This morning, I was being taken away to be sold into slavery... I called for help from the guards by the town gates, but they only smiled and ignored me, all while chatting with the kidnappers..."

"What...did you say...?" the governor breathlessly responded, recoiling in a grand fashion. He had to have heard that much already. This guy really knew how to play it up.

Or wait, maybe he really *was* freaking out now that he'd realized that one of the victims was from a foreign earl's household. I mean, yeah, that'd be pretty bad for him.

"Right before I was spirited away forever, the Goddess appeared and shouted, 'How dare you try to make slaves of such cute girls!' before delivering divine punishment to the kidnappers."

"Th-Then, what happened with the Goddess afterward?!"

"After speaking with me a little, she went back up there," I replied, giving the governor the answer I'd already thought up beforehand.

"Hrm... But are you sure the guards were in league with these criminals? Perhaps they just didn't notice your cries for help?"

"I broke through the lid of the barrel I was in and yelled for help right in front of them. If they didn't notice that, then they'd probably also let an entire enemy army march straight through the front gates. Is that the sort of rumor you want spreading about them?"

The governor fell silent. There was no way he could claim the guards weren't involved in the crime now.

"I'd say that the guards earned the wrath of the Goddess serves as proof more than anything, wouldn't you?"

The governor could only reluctantly nod, as shouts of agreement came from the crowd around us. I didn't know if he truly wanted to make it so that the guards were seen to have nothing to do with this, but now he'd completely lost the chance to say the soldiers weren't at all to blame.

"According to the kidnappers, their buyers were regional governors and middle-class traders. They weren't dealing with royalty or high-ranking nobles, or even the bigger merchants."

"...What was that?"

The color began returning to the governor's face. If those types of people were involved, things would get very complicated, very quickly. It could unravel into a scandal that shook the very foundation of the country. Worst-case scenario, those in power could try to push the blame onto whoever was in charge of the town where this had happened—in other words, the governor.

But if the culprits were lower-class aristocrats or slightly well-off merchants, then it was up to the royal family to decide whether to wipe them out or not. There wasn't anything the governor could do directly about this, but it could be taken care of, so long as he went the proper channels.

More than anything else, the ones at fault were the aristocrats and merchants trying to buy the little girls. If the governor arrested the guards responsible for facilitating such sales, then instead of this being a black mark for him, he'd be perceived as on the side of justice. If he cooperated in exposing the other corrupt governors, he might even earn the favor of the king himself.

He's probably seeing the light at the end of the tunnel by now, so I'll just give him one more push...

"Also, I'm supposed to pass along a message from the Goddess Celestine..."

"Wh-Wh... WHAAATTTTTT?!"

Not just the governor, but everyone within earshot let out a cry of astonishment. Clergymen and even the pope themselves would rarely get a chance to hear the words of the Goddess, so I could see why a simple governor receiving an honor as great as this would come as a shock (even if it was just me giving it to them as a message).

But considering why she came down, there wasn't anyone here who'd think this was going to be good news. The look on the governor's face definitely made it seem like he was a little on edge about it.

All right, let's get to passing on this message then.

"She told me: 'It is absolutely outrageous that these men kidnapped poor, innocent girls and sold them as slaves. The kidnappers, as well as those who took bribes to turn a blind eye, all bear the same sin. Give them all the harshest of punishments for their crimes. If not, I shall dole out the punishment myself.' That's what she said, but..."

"But...?"

I figured I'd take the chance to put the fear of the Goddess into the governor.

"Lady Celestine isn't a very detailed-oriented goddess, you see. She doesn't really care about each and every human, unless it's someone she's *really* taken by. When she mentioned 'punishment,' she meant that she'd flatten an entire estate if it meant taking out a single, irritating kidnapper hiding there, or maybe engulf all of Selinas in a sea of flames to destroy the kidnapping ring at its roots."

"Wh-What...?"

All the color drained from the governor's face. Everyone else who'd gathered around had also turned white as ghosts.

"Wh-Wh-Wh-Wh-Wh..."

It almost sounded like the governor was practicing his beatboxing. He was probably trying to force out either, "What should we do?" or, "Why?"

I think I'll go ahead and reassure him a little.

"There's need to worry. All you have to do is make sure to catch every single person involved in that kidnapping ring, from underlings to ringleaders, and that should be the end of it. Just arrest them all and make it so they can't kidnap or sell anyone into slavery ever again, and you're done."

"B-B-B-B... But..."

I'm gonna go out on a limb and guess he's trying to say, "But what if we can't?"

"All you have to do is put the pressure on the members of the kidnapping ring you already captured and make them spill the beans on everyone and everything they know: their fellow kidnappers, their bosses, where they were supposed to send all of us, where they've sold slaves before...all of it. If you can arrest the ones who bought those slaves and bring those children back to their parents, the Goddess might be willing to forgive you for missing an underling or two. *Might* be willing..."

This was an order from the Goddess herself, so the royal family should be willing to throw everything they had into helping out, as well. There was no room to question whether it was true or not. There were already so many direct witnesses, and there had to have been plenty more who'd heard the explosions and who'd seen the golden clouds.

Not to mention that they were dealing with a Goddess who was ready to squash not only a territory or two, but an entire *country*, in order to destroy the kidnapping ring down to the foundations. No connections or bribes could save them now. The only road left for those involved with the kidnappings was the one that led to their downfall.

"A-Arrest them! Arrest every last one of those men on the ground and tie them up! We're going to make them spill everything they know! Don't let them escape or try to off themselves! Failure will not be tolerated—it's not allowed!"

The lives of everyone who lived here were at risk—including the governor's own—so I could see why he was so desperate.

Oh yeah, I wonder if that little "present" I left behind a while ago is working its magic right about now...

"Mr. Governor, the Goddess said she'd let us know the location of the kidnappers' hideout by marking it with red smoke. I think she said it was somewhere in the slums..."

I was, of course, referring to the "parting gift" I'd left behind before the kidnappers took us away. I made it so it'd release a sleeping gas that would instantly knock anyone caught in it right out. After it did that job, it was set to incrementally release more and more red smoke. If everything had gone according to plan, the kidnappers there should all be knocked out cold right about now, and red smoke should be rising from the house they'd turned into their hideout.

It wasn't like it was a billowing pillar of smoke or anything, but it should be easy enough to find if you were looking for it. This was the first town I'd visited in this country, and I'd been shoved down into a barrel when they tried to spirit me away, so I wouldn't be able to lead anyone back to the house they'd kept me in. The smoke was just my own way of finding it again later. It should all work out in the end, as long as they made the other kidnappers cough up what they knew, but this was all "just in case" on my part.

"...Get going!"

"Right away!"

At the governor's orders, one of the higher-ranking soldiers formed up about half of the guards gathered here before rushing back into town.

As I watched them go, I saw a different group approaching from the exact opposite direction the soldiers were heading in. They looked to be local people and . were being led by a handful of different soldiers.

Ah... Those must be the families of the children that had gone missing.

Just as I'd predicted, the soldiers that swapped places with the ones who left for the slums had brought the families who were believed to have lost children to the kidnapping ring.

"Litheresa!"

"Sara!"

"Charlise! Where are you, Charlise?!"

"Yusef! Yuseeef!"

"Mommy!"

"Mother!"

Four calls to four different children, yet only two responses. This wasn't the first kidnapping incident, and there were plenty of other reasons why children might have gone missing, criminal or otherwise. Two of the families embraced their children, while the other two desperately searched to find their own. They clambered onto the back of the wagon, almost half-crazed as they went through the empty barrels. The crowd could only stare at the ground in silence when faced with the cruel difference between the two scenes.

Judging by the name they'd called, it sounded like the fourth family was looking for a boy. The kidnappers had only set their sights on cute little girls this time, but they may have gone after boys in the past. After being sold, they must be alive and well wherever they were now, and when they were finally found, they'd be able to see their families once more. That was what I wanted to believe.

"Governor…"

"I know! I know…" the governor said through gritted teeth as he furrowed his brow, already guessing at what I wanted to say.

I'll put my faith in the governor here. If anyone can take care of it, he can.

After some time had passed, the four families returned to town; two of them smiling and laughing, the other two silent, eyes cast to the ground.

The only one left here was a five- to six-year-old girl, standing all by herself.

"Huh?"

After some back-and-forth, I learned that Layette was six years old, the youngest child of a family of five out in the countryside, and had been sold by her parents. Apparently, this sort of thing happened all the time. Since human trafficking was a serious crime, it had been done under the guise of "long-term indentured servitude," and they'd paid her wages up front for a term of eighty years.

She was supposed to at least be treated like a person that way, but, in reality, it was the exact same as being an actual slave. While she was being taken to her buyer, she'd been kidnapped, instead.

"So…what happens in a situation like this?" I asked.

She'd already been sold, so of course there were going to be problems if they tried returning her to her parents. The buyer might be thinking that she'd run away and would come after them, seeking compensation. Most worrying of all, though, was that these were the type of parents who sold their child for a profit. There was a chance they'd just end up selling her to another buyer.

"I wonder?" the governor pondered aloud. When you think about it, he probably wasn't as well-versed in this sort of thing.

The governor called up one of his subordinates and asked him the same question in my stead.

"Her parents signed a contract and received payment, so they have no right to take her back. If we were to return her to them, with no strings attached, there's a chance it could lead to strife between the other jealous families who let their children go in the same way. There's also the possibility that they could end up selling their own child once again..."

"So what you're saying is that it's impossible to return her to her parents... No, that it's not in her best interests to do so."

"Exactly, sir. Also, there's the matter of the person who bought— uh, I mean, *paid* for her services. Not only is this entirely against her wishes, but this is a suspect agreement at best, one that's extremely similar to outright human trafficking," the subordinate explained. "That's why they won't want anyone to know that they were involved in this. They won't submit a claim for damages, and will most likely cut their losses after not being able to receive the girl they paid for, rather than risk this blowing up in their face. I would imagine that they have already left town and are heading to their next destination by now. In short, trying to find and deliver her to her contractor would not only be extremely difficult, but not in her best interests whatsoever."

"Then what's going to happen to the child?"

"The best option would be to send her to an orphanage," the subordinate answered. "I'm sure she would be much happier that way, rather dying an early death living in the slums. It's a very difficult institution to get into, but I would imagine it to not be a problem if you gave the order."

Layette listened to the discussion between the governor and his subordinate, eyes cast downward. It looked like she knew what that meant. I could see her shaking.

"Very well, then I'll write to them later. She's a child saved by the Goddess, so I'm sure they'll take good care of her there. All that's left is—"

"Hold on a minute!"

Before I knew it, the words had forced their way out of my mouth.

"I'll take her myself!"

"What?!"

Everyone was surprised to hear that, but the ones who'd actually vocalized their shock were Roland and the others.

"M-Miss Kaoru, you can't!" Francette said, balking.

"That may be a bit too much to ask for..." Roland agreed.

Belle and Emile, on the other hand, didn't comment on my decision. They thought of me as the goddess to whom they'd sworn their eternal loyalty. It felt like that loyalty was weighing a little heavier on me lately... Not to mention, they were orphans themselves. They'd lived their lives scrounging around in the streets, being treated as less than human.

"Is there a problem with that?" I asked, turning to the governor and his subordinate.

228

There certainly wouldn't be any problems from my companions. They'd probably give in if I pressed hard enough. And if they didn't? Then I'd just have to tell them it wasn't working out and we'd have to go our separate ways. That wasn't a threat, I'll have you know, just a clear declaration of my will.

"I don't see any problem with it," the subordinate answered. "Not only is she a kidnapping victim, but there is no feasible way to deliver her to her contractor, since they essentially abandoned her. I would say that they also abandoned their right to have her work under them, in the process. They haven't even fulfilled the bare minimum for their duty to take care of her, after all. Any abusive treatment or negligence regarding those duties makes the contract null and void. I'm sure that the contractor won't be able to claim anything, now that someone else had to go through the trouble of saving her, even if that was through the powers of the Goddess herself. The only problem left is what the girl wishes to do, now that she is free. She can either return to her parents, go to the orphanage, live in the slums, pick a completely new way to live her life...or choose to go with you. Personally, I wouldn't recommend the slums or returning to her parents..."

The governor nodded, satisfied after hearing the explanation.

"What do you wanna do?" I asked Layette.

Looking up at me, she smiled from ear-to-ear and clung to my arm. "I'll come with you!"

All right, got myself a little girl! Now I don't have to feel all bummed out when hanging around these two couples!

"Then that settles that!"

"This settles nothing!"

I ignored Francette's remarks. I had picked up the ability to ignore nagging complaints like that from my time working at my company back on Earth, but I never thought it'd come in handy here.

Just in case, I asked the governor to write up a report on what had happened with Layette, mainly as a way to prove her identity, which made her officially free and recognized as a citizen of his territory. I had him sign the papers saying that I'd be her legal guardian, and, well, that really was that. I provided the paper and writing utensils to make it happen, but the subordinate was the one who wrote everything up. All the governor did was offer his signature to make it official.

Normally, the governor would never go out of his way to get these types of documents ready and sign off on them. I didn't know if he felt sorry for poor Layette, after everything she'd been through, or if it was maybe because he didn't want to risk being unkind to a girl personally saved by the Goddess, but…okay, I was pretty sure it was the latter. I'd be willing to bet a gold coin on it, in fact.

Pretty sure I wouldn't find anyone to take me up on that one, either.

This way, Layette wouldn't have anything to worry about, even if we did run into the person who had bought her contract. If they ever tried coming after her, all we had to do was show them the documents and make a commotion to get the local officials to help her out. If we told them we were going to look into the original contract, to see if it actually constituted human trafficking or not, I was pretty sure they'd back off for good.

On the other hand, if we ever ended up running into Layette's parents, they wouldn't be able to take her away if she didn't want them to. They'd already sold her off to line their own pockets, so they wouldn't be able to demand that they raise her themselves, or for her to hand over all the money she'd saved up. In fact, she had the right to demand that *they* give *her* back the money they'd received in advance for her eighty years of indentured servitude. That money belonged to Layette, not her parents. It should be easy to chase them away if we brought that up and shoved it in their faces. They could end up forced into slavery themselves, if they were convicted of human trafficking, so they'd definitely want to avoid getting any officials involved.

What if Layette wanted to go back to her parents, you ask? She was a free girl, and that was her choice to make. No one should be able to dictate how someone else lived their life.

"I suppose I'll be on my way, then."

"W-Wait! Wait, please!"

I was ready to leave after finishing my business here, but the governor stopped me. Well, I really couldn't say that I hadn't expected this to happen. Even *I'd* try to stop me if I was in his position.

It'd be hard to just up and leave after everything that just happened, and I'd feel bad snubbing the governor when I owed him for signing the papers that guaranteed Layette her freedom (even if it was his subordinate who wrote them).

I guess I can humor him a little longer...

"What is it?" I asked.

The governor straightened himself up, face stiff, before turning to Roland. "I would like to invite you to my estate. May I trouble you to come there with me?"

The governor suddenly seemed much more formal, compared to how commanding he'd been up until now. It was true that I'd introduced ourselves as being members of an earl's family, but the governor's status meant that he far and away outranked us. Besides, I only *looked* young enough to be a child. This was *his* territory, and it wasn't like we were ambassadors on a courtesy call, so he'd naturally be brusque with someone so much younger than he was. I was sure that the guy had plenty to keep himself occupied at the moment, so I'd say we were pretty lucky to have him take the time to handle Layette's situation, when this was the first time we'd actually met.

The reason he suddenly became so polite with us was because he *needed* to be polite. To be specific, it was probably because he needed a favor. It was a delicate situation for him, and he was walking a fine line; either this could end up a horrible disaster, or it could be the chance he didn't know he'd been waiting for. I was a cute, foreign, aristocratic girl, who'd not only been directly saved by the Goddess, but had spoken with her as well.

Yeah, I said cute girl. *That thing with the kidnappers proved it to be the* de facto *truth. It ain't like they did it as a joke, that's for sure! I might be able to pull that out as some kinda trump card later, if anyone tries to argue otherwise...*

Roland turned to look at me, uncertain of how to answer, so I went ahead and did it for him. Again.

"No, we actually need to hurry up and get moving. I only met with the Goddess for a few moments, and I've already told you everything she had to say, so I believe we're done here."

It made sense for me to tell them everything I knew about the kidnappers and the Goddess, since I'd been there when it happened. However, it seemed like the governor thought Roland was the one who decided what we'd do next, so his eyes had flown open wide when I answered instead.

All right, time to make sure he knows that he won't be getting Roland to convince me otherwise.

"By the way, *I'm* the one who has the last say in what we do for our little group. Father assigned *me* as the one to watch over them, after all. My brother's never been able to go against what I say. Ohoho…"

That was the story we'd all decided on beforehand, but Roland still didn't look too happy about it.

Though he seemed taken aback by the sudden turn of events, the governor seemed to have caught on to what that meant. I'd heard plenty of stories of aristocratic brothers who couldn't help but dote on their little sisters, so this shouldn't be all that strange for him to hear about now.

"Now, now, don't say that… There's still so much I want to ask about the kidnappers. I'd also like to confirm what the Goddess told you one more time, at least. You said you're traveling around our country, did you not? I believe there's plenty I can teach you about Drisard, as well."

I thought he might try something like that, so I decided to let him have the finishing blow that I'd prepared beforehand:

"Well, I had so much free time waiting for you to arrive that I went ahead and wrote everything down that the Goddess said regarding the kidnapping ring. Here you are." I pulled out a few sheets of paper as I said as much. "Learning everything there is to know about this country would take the fun out of the journey itself. I'd rather we took our time to experience it all for ourselves. You wouldn't be able to call it "studying" otherwise, no?"

I kept plenty of paper and writing utensils in reserve at all times, just for situations like these. I also made sure to write down that the Goddess said to not push things too far trying to catch everyone in the kidnapping syndicate. No torturing people or forcing confessions out of them, no sentencing innocent people; you know, things like that. Things could get real ugly real fast if I didn't specify that.

"What…?" The governor's mouth hung open as he stood there in a daze, reflexively taking the papers I pushed onto him.

"We'll be heading out now! For real this time!"

Before the governor could think up another excuse to keep us here, I'd already taken Layette and headed over to where Ed was waiting. Ed was kind enough to catch on to what was going on, and crouched down so I could get myself and Layette on his back. With that, we'd finally made it through another sticky situation.

"Hi ho, Silver!"

"Them again?! Just who is this "Silver" horse, dang it!"

Ed made his displeasure known, as per usual, when I did this. Guess I couldn't just tell him to get off his high horse…

Heh. Heheh.

Ed began slowly trotting along, in complete contrast to my spirited shout just now, but I could understand why. Usually, I'd be on the verge of getting bucked off if Ed ran too fast, but Layette didn't even have the proper riding gear on. In fact, I'd bet that this was her first time even riding a horse.

Since I was already on the move, Francette and the others weren't going to just hang around here, either. Everyone quickly saddled up and followed after me.

"Ah! W-Wait…"

The governor tried his best to stop us, but it was already too late.

"Good luck trying to catch those kidnappers! Do your best to not make the Goddess angry with you, either!" I turned around and shouted behind me. When I did, I caught a glimpse of the governor shouting orders to his underlings.

They wouldn't try and force us to do anything now; the risks for doing so would be enormous. We were supposed to be part of a foreign noble's family, with Roland as the apparent heir to the family name, and me as the daughter who everyone doted on. The Goddess supposedly didn't care all that much about human lives, but she had gone out of her way to save two of the girls traveling with this group. The consequences if anything happened would be...terrifying, to say the least.

"Why would you do something like that, Kaoru? If you're going to bring up the Goddess, wouldn't things go over more smoothly if you just told them you're her messenger?" Francette asked once we'd put some distance between us and the town gates.

It seemed she'd finally settled on being casual with me again after everything that had happened, though she still couldn't bring herself to descend to the same level that Emile and the others used with me. I mean, I *was* supposed to be her "little sister-in-law," since she was Roland's fiancée, so she should be at least a *little* informal with me. As for me, I'd call her "Francette," or "Fran," depending on how I was feeling at the time.

I didn't really mind what she called me. What I *did* mind was the question that she'd just asked.

"If I said that, they'd just try even *harder* to stop us! They'd send people to shadow us, and if word spread to other people about it, then things would spiral out of control!"

"Ah..."

It seemed that Francette wanted other people to pay their respects to me, as well, since I was supposed to be a goddess. I couldn't just come out and tell people that, of course, which was why she was urging me to announce that I was an angel, or a messenger, or whatever. But it looked like she finally realized why that would've been a bad thing.

…I wonder if it's about time to move on and give this a shot?

"Ed, there's something I wanna ask you…"

"Whatcha being all formal for all of a sudden? I owe you my life, missy, so I'm ready to do whatever you say!"

"Thanks! I knew I could count on you. Actually, I wanted to ask you to pull the wagon…"

"LIKE HELL I WILL!!!" Ed exploded.

That's not what you were saying just a second ago!

"I-I'm a purebred horse meant for riding! I'm a proud, prestigious, military horse bred for war! And those other horses? They're the elite of the elite, bred and raised to be used by royalty, and you're telling us to pull a wagon?! I know it's you who's asking, missy, but I'm not going to let that happen!"

He was actually mad… His wife and daughter seemed pretty put off by the whole thing, as well. I never knew this sort of thing was so important to horses… Maybe it was kinda like the difference between a fighter pilot and an airline pilot? I mean, I like to think that they both have pretty important jobs, but…

Oh, but it's not like Roland or Francette's horses have anything to do with this, huh.

"Their horses don't matter, right?"

"Huh?"

"You're the only one who'd be pulling the wagon."

"WHAT?!" Ed's jaw practically hit the floor.

"J-Just me? I'm the only one who's going to be pulling this whole cart?"

Roland and Francette's horses watched him with pity in their eyes.

"B-But this isn't just about me. I was thinking how this is going to be hard on poor Layette if she has to keep going on like this, is all…"

236

"*Mgh...*"

Being a six-year-old on horseback for this extended road trip had to be hard on the girl. We didn't have the luxury of saddles in this world like back on modern-day Earth, so all we'd do was drape a cloth over the horse's back and throw a cushion on top. Aside from that, we only had a belt and some cords keeping us strapped in, purely so we wouldn't fall off. I only had a belt and cords for myself, though, and Layette was just hanging on to me. There was a fairly high chance that she could fall off Ed if something shook us hard enough.

Horse riding also gets to you...mostly in the butt, hips, and groin. It really messes with your stomach until you get used to it, too. Even now, after I'd had some time to get used to riding, it was still doing a number on me when I wasn't potion doping. Ed had already heard how much I complained and cried when I was trying to get used to it without using potions, which was probably why he realized it must be much worse for a little girl like Layette.

"*B-But...*"

Looks like the only way I'm going to convince him is to bring out the wagon and twist his arm—er, leg—until he agrees...

"Hold up for a second, everyone!"

Now, how should I convince Ed to do this...

"Come forth, war chariot of the Goddess!"

As I chanted the magic words, a small carriage appeared at my command—or, more accurately, a potion container in the shape of a wagon.

There was a small tank filled with a potion inside. It was a four-wheeler, but shrunk down to be more compact. This was no ordinary wagon, but one that was used for battle and in times of war: a chariot. I didn't make it as small as the ones from that one movie, but a

237

slightly larger type with four wheels. It was way smaller than your average cart and was specially built from a custom mix of titanium and FRP (fiber-reinforced plastic).

FRP was a lightweight material which boasted the greatest strength of all extant kinds of plastic. It was a reliable material, used in everything from ships to airplanes, and even in race cars.

It'd be no easy task trying to fix the chariot in this world if it was ever damaged—if you weren't me. All I had to do was shove the broken one into my Item Box and make a new one. I could just break the old one down and use it for something else.

"Wh-What in the world…"

Ed and the others had eyes as wide as dinner plates. Everyone here was used to me putting stuff into my Item Box or taking things out of it. They all knew me as a goddess from another world, so it wasn't anything to be surprised about now. What did surprise them was how incredible the cart I'd conjured from thin air was. Though it was small, it still managed to fit four wheels onto it. Two wheels would make it rough to handle, due to how uneven the front and back would end up being, which was why I went with four instead.

I made it without a roof, having the sides come up to about chest height to keep anyone from falling out. There was a windshield made of acrylic attached to the front, and the wheels were on the bigger side to improve its drivability. The back wheels stuck out toward the sides more, however, which meant the front and back wheels ended up overlapping with each other somewhat, due to how small it was. I also made the seats sit pretty high up, so it'd be easier to talk with anyone who was still on horseback. But, just in case things got dicey, all it took was one pull of a lever to make the seats lower and a titanium shutter pop out from the sides to cover us.

"And that's not all..."

I gestured for Francette to back away a little before I pulled a lever on the chariot.

KA-THUNK!

Two sets of double-edged blades sprung out from either side.

"Huh?" Everyone and the horses were stunned.

"I said it was a *war* chariot, didn't I? Layette and I can't fight, so it has to have some combat potential of its own. This isn't a chariot meant for warriors to ride, but something to fight with. That's why it's not the people riding it who fight, but the chariot and the horse pulling it, instead."

I pulled on it to show off how light it was. It sported an open-top design and cut an impressive figure, no matter what angle you looked at it from, and it was compact and lightweight to boot. The horse who pulled it wouldn't be any normal grunt, but a proud warrior bred and raised for battle.

"The horse who pulls this chariot will be known as a warrior of the Goddess. They shall carry the title of 'Sacred Horse,' and their name will be carried on for generations..."

"*I will gladly accept that duty!*"

"Huh?"

Roland's horse had cut me off before I could finish my speech.

"*If Ed doesn't wish to do it, then I will gladly take the role. I only ask that he carry my master in my stead.*"

"*No, allow me to handle it,*" Francette's horse spoke up. "*I believe it would be better for Sir Ed to carry Master Francette instead. It should be much easier on him, since she's so much lighter.*"

"*Hold on...*"

Ed was completely taken aback. While they may have been proud royal horses, they still both paid their due respects to Ed. Not only was he older than them, but he was the horse of a goddess, and they respected him as the head of his family...though they may have just been after Ed's daughter.

This was their chance to take on the honor of being one of the goddess's mounts and to earn the title of "Sacred Horse," the steed who was tasked with pulling her war chariot. They weren't about to let it pass them by.

"Hmm, what to do, what to do... If Ed doesn't want to, I guess I might take you up on that. Roland, Francette, are you guys okay with that?"

"All I heard was a bunch of neighing from you and the horses, so I have no idea what in the world you're asking us for..." came Roland's weary reply.

He had a point there. I was the only one who could speak horse, after all.

"W-Wait wait wait! Hold on just a second here!"

Ed seemed to be getting desperate now, but I still continued the conversation.

"Then either of you would be fine, really..."

"I said hold your dang horses!!!" Ed shouted as loud as he could.

Yup, that should do it.

I retracted the blades on the war chariot—actually, let's just call it a wagon when it's in normal mode. It'd be a pain to explain why it could do all this if anyone found out about it.

Ed was in high spirits as he pulled the wagon along. I'd already told the horses about how I was a goddess (or was pretending to be one, at least). Everyone else already saw me that way, so I wanted to make sure the horses knew, as well. I mean, they *are* horses, so I shouldn't have to worry about them leaking information to anyone.

Still, Ed didn't really see himself as a "Sacred Horse," or as the "horse of a goddess," or anything like that. He worked hard, and he was grateful to me for saving his life and for buying him the mare he'd had his eye on. That had been enough for me. It was only in that one moment, when he saw how the other horses were champing at the bit to take the job, that he came to realize the honor of the position. He despaired at the thought that they might take it from him.

"This is so much lighter than I thought it'd be. Is this actually made out of some sturdy stuff, missy? It's not going to break apart if we suddenly come under attack, and I have to gallop away at full speed, right?"

"Don't worry, it's made of something lighter than iron but stronger than wood, so it should be able to take a bit of extra stress without breaking. Just think of it as some sort of divine metal from the gods. That said, it *will* fall apart if we put too much pressure on it."

"Understood. I guess I'll try to keep the galloping to a minimum, then."

Even if it was light, that was only compared to other lightweight wagons. Who knew how fast this thing could go with only one horse pulling it.

Ah, Layette looked kinda overwhelmed by how much I'd been talking with Ed. I guess I would be, too, if the person who'd just adopted me was whinnying back and forth with their horse this much. No one wanted to leave their future in the hands of someone who seemed like they had a few screws loose...

Wait, is she starting to regret coming with me now? Oh crap, I have to explain this away somehow!

"U-Um, just so you know, this is…uh…"

"Y-You can talk to horses?! That's so amazing!"

Oh, would you look at that. She wasn't freaked out, just plain surprised. She was going to find out that I was (pretending to be) a goddess sooner or later, so it might be a good idea to just tell her now and get it over with. I didn't want her to freak out about it if she found out when there were other people around.

Right, now, how should I explain this…

"Huh?!"

Yup, looks like that came as a shock to her, too.

"Y-Y-You're a *goddess*?! I-I mean, you were already a goddess to me when you said you would take me in, b-but I never thought you'd be a *real* goddess!"

Layette's eyes were practically shining.

…Uh-oh. I knew what these were. These were the same eyes Emile and Belle had when they looked at me. They were the eyes of a fanatic.

Those two were enough for me as is! I didn't want another fanatic. I just wanted healing! Yes, that's right! Healing! In the form of little girls!

"Th-This is a big secret, okay, Layette? I told you because I think you're a good girl who can keep that secret, so you can't tell anyone about this. Everyone here already knows, but we don't know who's listening, so you can't talk about it when there're other people around. I'm just pretending to be Roland's little sister, so let's keep it that way, okay?"

"B-But that's so cool…"

I guess it's no use trying to convince a little girl to consider the big picture, huh…

That's when Francette stepped in. "Let's pretend you were a goddess, Layette. If everyone tried to serve and worship you all the time, and you didn't have anyone you could talk normally with, do you think you would have any fun?"

"No…"

"Would it be fun to have aristocrats and other rich people coming to you every day, fighting with each other to have you make their wishes come true?"

"…No."

"Then you know what you have to do, right?"

"Yeah!"

All right, way to go Francette and your sagely wisdom! You aren't in your thirties for nothing! Even though your body is about twenty years old, thanks to me!

But thinking about it, I should technically be twenty-seven (mentally, at least) while my physical age was around nineteen… Well, it should be that way, but here I was, still stuck in my fifteen-year-old body. You know what, I wasn't going to think too hard about that anymore.

Anyway, I should be able to talk with Layette normally now. Let's get started with that healing time I'd been waiting for…

"Please feel free to order me to do anything you want, Lady Kaoru."

Eh?

"Wh-Why are you talking like that? I thought you weren't going to treat me like a goddess or anything…"

"I thought this would be the right way to talk with you, since you're an aristocrat and all."

Ahhhhhh, that's right! Crap, I totally forgot about that! Layette's a commoner and I'm supposed to be the daughter of an aristocrat. There's no way she would talk normally with me!

Wh-What do I do... My precious healing time is slipping through my fingers...

"All right, then you're my sister! From now on, you're my little sister, Layette!"

"Huh?!"

I know she didn't look like an aristocrat at all, but I was just going to do the same thing I did with Emile and say she was another child our father had with a servant, but we still got along great! It was all I had left!

"That takes care of that!" I shouted to the others gathered around the wagon.

Roland and Francette weren't surprised in the slightest, as if they'd been expecting it to come to this. Emile and Belle also had nothing to add, since they'd never go against anything I said in the first place.

With that, Layette became my little sister—without her getting a say in the matter at all.

After spending a night in a small village and another night roughing it out in the wild, we finally made it to a decently large town. I hadn't planned on staying that long in a town so close to the border, but I shouldn't have to worry about Brancott anymore, now that we were this far away.

Instead of rushing along, I was going to have us stay a bit longer in town so I could work on finding some guys who were suitable marriage material. That was why I was going on this journey in the first place, after all, so I didn't really have a reason to rush.

"We'll go ahead and stay here for a while." I decided to have everyone stop so I could talk with them before we went into town.

"Do we have something to do here, Big Sis?" Layette asked, tilting her head to the side.

Sh-She's so cute!!!

We'd decided that "Big Sis" was Layette's official nickname for me, and everyone else could call me by name if they needed to. When we were alone or didn't have to worry about getting our stories mixed up, she would just call me her "Big Sis," and she'd call Belle and Francette her sisters as well. I couldn't help but wonder why I was the only one she called her "big" sister, though…not that it really mattered.

"Well, you see, the whole point of this trip is for me to find someone to marry, and—"

"Huh?"

Layette's expression of disbelief cut me off before I could finish, probably because it came as a shock that a goddess would be looking for someone to get hitched to.

"You have a bunch of scary big brothers and sisters who seem like they'd chase away any boy who gets close to you… Is there any guy who would try and see an aristocrat's daughter when she's staying at an inn? Do you even have a chance to talk with other boys and stuff?"

…

…

…

…

"GAHHH! HOW DID I NOT REALIZE THAAAAAAT?!"

"That's why it's time for a change of strategy." I had to make sure to tell everyone of my new plan.

"I've come to realize that there's a *slight* problem with me trying to pass myself off as an aristocrat's daughter. I can't just go dating any normal boys right off the bat as a noble and, even if I do find another aristocratic boy, there'll be serious problems once they realize I'm only pretending to be high-class. Even if Earl Adan is letting us say we're part of his family, I don't have any proof that I'm a bona fide aristocrat or anything..."

Roland cut in. "Not only I am royalty, but I hold the title of duke, as well. Francette earned the status of viscount due to her efforts from the war, so it's not a lie to say that *we're* nobility, at least. So long as you don't claim to be part of the aristocracy yourself and I say you're my little sister, no one should be able to accuse you of lying. If it comes down to it, we can just say we're siblings-in-law, so it should all work out fine. And like I've said before, just say the word and I'll tell Balmore to give you an official title. How does being an earl—no, a marchioness—sound?"

It was a pretty normal thing for royals to have a bunch of different titles. It came in handy if they ever needed to blend in with the nobility, if they ever needed to travel incognito, or if they wanted to distance themselves from their royal heritage.

Francette had already been given the title of viscount, too. I bet they wanted to make her look better, status-wise, if she was going to marry the brother of the king. But even without doing so, Francette was a hero of the war, who'd received not only a holy blade but the official title of Protector of the Goddess. There wasn't anyone who could object to her engagement with Roland.

"...I'll pass, thanks."

Despite that, I promptly turned down Roland's proposition. He'd asked me over and over again throughout the years following the war and after Celes had descended, but I refused him every time. Roland was the type of guy who would sulk over every little thing like this, too.

If I became a noble of Balmore, it'd mean the king and his ministers could come to me with their demands and stuff, so I could definitely see why he'd want that to happen. I bet they weren't *actually* thinking of doing so, but I'd at least have to show my face before the king. That, and I'd become a pretty powerful asset that they could lord over other countries.

"Grah… Well, if you ever feel like having a title, just let me know. It should only take about three extra minutes to finalize the paperwork, on top of the round trip by horse to get it signed."

So he's already prepared for it to happen anytime?! Good lord, man! I don't wanna be saddled with anything as annoying as being an aristocrat. I ain't about to get tied down by status and start governing the people who live on my land, or any other junk that might get pushed on me. Actually, I bet that's why they want me to go through with it. I just want to enjoy living my life, free to do whatever I want, thank you very much!

Putting all that aside, I went ahead and got to the point: "That's why I want us to split up from here on out."

"WHAAAAAAT?!"

Yeah, I guess they'd be kinda shocked to hear that all of a sudden.

"But if that happens, I won't be able to get in the way of you marrying someone from another coun—" Roland let slip before he could catch himself. "N-Nevermind…"

"…What did you… WHAT DID YOU JUST SAAAAAAY?!"

I never thought there'd be a filthy TRAITOR in my party, damn it!!!

My words were met with fierce opposition from the group. But of course they'd be opposed. Layette was even bonking me on the chest with her fists, tears in her eyes.

I don't have much cushioning there, so that kinda hurts... Argh, shut up, me!

"Don't worry, you and I are still sticking together, Layette."

"Okay, then I agree! Let's all split up!" she beamed, the complete opposite of how she was mere seconds ago.

Frickin' kids, I tell ya...

"Of course we're not going to let you do that! You just got yourself kidnapped the other day, remember?! And easily, at that!" Roland fired back.

"I *let* myself get captured so I could save all those girls and take down the kidnapping ring in one fell swoop! Did you guys even come save me when that happened? Did you do *anything* for me then? Hmm?"

"Ngh..."

It was a breeze to shoot down his argument. If it came down to it, I could just say I was a goddess, so I'd never really be in danger, and he wouldn't be able to say anything about it.

Francette, Emile, and Belle, on the other hand, all looked like they didn't know how to handle this. They probably didn't know what to say, because they were torn between wanting to stay with me and following my orders because they'd sworn their loyalty to me.

...Sorry about that, guys.

"Wouldn't it be fine if we all just acted like commoners, then?" Roland suggested.

"There's no way you'd ever pass as a commoner! All it'd take is, like, two seconds of talking with you and anyone could figure it out. You only know what it's like to be royalty, after all, so it's not like you could follow the conversation or anything... And if you *were* pretending to be a commoner, then you wouldn't be carrying around a sword unless you were a soldier or a hired guard or something. It'd be weird to have a commoner like me be surrounded by my own entourage of bodyguards. Just having you around is going to mess with my soul searching, Roland. Way more than you know..."

It's true, Roland was a hunk. That didn't mean he just had a good face or anything, though. He was someone who gave off an abundant aura of charm and masculine sex appeal. No boy would dare get close to me with him around...

"I'm not telling you to go back home or anything. Though, I wouldn't really mind if you did..."

"But what are you going to do...?"

"I'm thinking it's time we drop the sibling act, so I can think up a new background story."

"Leave it to us!" Emile, Belle, and Fran all responded in unison.

"We're commoners, so there shouldn't be any problems with us coming with you," Emile said, with Belle nodding in agreement.

"Sir Roland would stick out like a sore thumb, but I should be fine, since I was born and raised a commoner as well!"

"Huh...?"

"F-Fran... That's, uh, you know..." Roland couldn't hide his shock over Francette's sudden betrayal.

"I already swore my loyalty to you, Mi— Kaoru! Of course I'd be coming with you!"

Roland fell to his knees in utter disbelief.

Fran, I know you stopped yourself from trying to be extra formal with me there, but that doesn't matter if you're just gonna come out and say you swore loyalty to me! That basically gives it away!

With Roland white as ash and at a loss for words, the rest of our group launched into a heated argument over what was going to happen next.

"It's dangerous for a group of children to be alone together. I absolutely *must* come along with you, since I'm an adult!"

"You say you're an adult, but you only look like you're about fifteen or sixteen at best. I already look older than you, so it shouldn't really make a difference if you're there or not. I'm already sixteen, so I'm an adult too. If we need an adult with wisdom, just having Kaoru around is plenty. Oh, and I'm not saying that it's better to not have you around, Fran. You know, just to make that clear."

"Mgh..." Fran's face screwed up in frustration as she found herself unable to refute Emile's words.

"We're coming with you, Kaoru. We'll be there to take care of you, and, if the time calls for it, we'll even become your shield."

Oof, laying it on a bit heavy there, Belle...

"Hm... I guess I *am* a little worried about it being just Layette and me..."

It wouldn't be a problem if it were just me, but it wasn't like I could stick around Layette the whole time. I guess I only had one choice here...

"Then leave her to us!" Belle cried out.

"I'll be counting on you guys, then."

"Okay!" came three separate replies.

"You're not coming with us, Fran."

"What?!" she shouted in disbelief.

"I mean, don't you feel kinda bad just leaving the poor guy alone?" I said, pointing to Roland, while he just stayed on the ground, slumped over in defeat. Fran sent a withering glance his way, looking annoyed.

Hey, Fran…he's still the brother of a king, y'know? And you totally looked up to him, remember?! You were acting like a high-school girl who just had some idol propose to her when you came to tell me! This is a pretty big about-face you're pulling…

"But you can't do anything by yourself, right, Roland? You always have someone helping you get dressed or tying your shoes…"

"I can do all of that just fine!" Roland howled, cutting me off.

In the end, we settled on Layette, Emile, Belle and I all being siblings, with me being the second oldest daughter. Roland and Francette were an engaged couple, who just happened to be staying at the same inn, and ultimately didn't have anything to do with us.

"I actually would've preferred you guys to stay at a separate inn, since I just feel like you're going to blow my cover…"

"We already decided this, so don't start complaining about it now!"

Francette would usually do whatever I said, but she wasn't going to give up on this one. I could understand why, though.

"Then let's get going. You two go do your own thing, and make sure you don't come over to chat with me or say anything that would give me away—especially you, Roland!"

Roland and Francette didn't look too stoked to hear that, but Layette, Emile, Belle and I headed straight for the town. I made sure to stow my chariot away in my Item Box first, though, with Layette and me both riding on Ed. Things could get messy if we pulled up to the inn with *that*.

As we trundled along, Emile and Belle matched our pace while keeping slightly behind us. It was the perfect spot to stay aware of their surroundings, while being ready to jump in and protect me at a moment's notice, should anything go wrong. Ed probably didn't find it particularly pleasant to be protected by his wife and child, but there wasn't much he could do about it, since I was the priority here and Ed knew it.

"Sorry about all this."

"Heh! That's my job, so don't mention it," came Ed's casual reply.

No, I wasn't surprised that Ed realized what I was talking about just now.

His job, huh... I wonder if horses expect a salary and stuff for work, too?

Roland and Francette were about fifty meters behind us when they finally entered the town. When my group and I were on the way to the center of town to look for an inn...

"Eek!"

...A wagon suddenly veered off to the side of the road to park by a store, smacking into a little girl. Though it looked like it only bumped her, the wagon was still made of metal and it could definitely hurt someone pretty badly. The girl had collapsed onto the stone pavement, groaning in pain. She still seemed conscious, but she might have fractured something if she'd hit the ground too hard. I didn't know if it was from the wagon or the stone pavement, but I could see marks and scratches on her cheek from where she had been hit.

"Ed!"

"Yes, ma'am!"

He trotted over to the girl and bent down slightly. I grabbed Layette and got off, setting her on the ground before pulling a potion from my Item Box. It'd be kinda shocking if I just made a potion on the spot out of thin air, after all. That was why, if I took it out of my Item Box, it would look like I was pulling it out of somewhere...that they couldn't see... Okay, sorry, the fact that it was going to shock people didn't really change, did it? It made *me* feel better about it, at least.

"Drink this!"

The girl was still conscious. She was so confused by what was happening that she reflexively took the potion from me and drank it down on the spot. Her pain and her wounds disappeared in an instant.

"Huh...?"

"Are you okay? I'm pretty sure your injuries are all better now, but your clothes are a little...ripped..."

The crowd around us was abuzz with talk, and I could hear the words "goddess" and "miracle" being thrown around.

O-Oh crap! I couldn't stop myself! It's pure reflex by now!

I was probably an open secret in Balmore, so they wouldn't really bat an eye if I did something like this there. That was how I'd lived my life the past four years, so I ended up casually giving out potions to any kids who were hurt without thinking too hard about it. It was pretty much just instinct at this point. But I just did this in a brand new town in a brand new country, which meant...

"G-Girl! Just who *are* you?!"

Of course a middle-aged aristocrat just stepped out of their carriage!

"Ed!"

"Roger that!"

Ed and I practically knew what the other was thinking after spending so much time together. He lowered himself down, and I clambered onto his back with Layette in tow.

"Let's get outta here!"

"Aye aye, ma'am!"

Though I still didn't have any modern-day riding gear on him, such as you'd find on Earth, I at least made sure he had a saddle and stirrups. I held on tight to Layette as we made our escape at full speed, alongside Emile and Belle, of course. Roland and Francette were pretending not to know us, following behind from a good distance away.

Hey, they might actually seem like people sent to chase after us.

The crowd was in an uproar behind me, and I could hear people yelling and stuff—but who cared about that now? All I was thinking about now was getting the hell out of here, and fast! If we didn't, they most likely *were* going to send people after us.

I put some distance between the town and myself before finally stopping and taking my chariot out of my Item Box. Pulling it out back there would have just made it *too* obvious who I really was. I hooked it up to Ed, then lifted Layette up into it, before jumping in myself. This should really let us haul ass to get outta here.

Ed and the others had already had plenty of potions to pump up their stamina and speed, so all it'd take was a little more doping and no horse should be able to catch us. They'd only seen us for a second, after all, and when they did we were riding off on three horses; they definitely wouldn't be looking for a wagon with four people accompanying it. We should be able to play it off without an issue if anyone tried to find us now.

"All right, let's get going!"

Roland had caught up to us by this point.

"...It's the perfect plan. Everyone will think I'm just a commoner."

Ngh!

"...and make sure you don't come over to chat with me or say anything that would give me away—especially you, Roland!"

Mngh... Nrrrgh...

"Heheh... Hahaha!"

MMMGGGHHHHHH!!!

"Ahahahaha!"

"Hehe..." Even Francette was getting in on this...

"Ahahahaha!!!"

Emile and Belle, you guys, too?! Gahhh, just kill me already!!!

Extra Chapter:
Much, Much Later...

"Mom!"

"Grandma!"

"Great-grandma…"

Surrounded by a group of my children and great-grandchildren, my consciousness was slowly slipping away from me. I lived a good life…but there was just *one* thing… There was one thing I couldn't forgive.

"Hey, God!"

"Y-Yes! I know, I know…"

A white space. In this empty void was a man with golden hair and blue eyes, who was the physical embodiment of what every woman would consider to be a "good man." He wore a white outfit that seemed like something an aristocrat from ancient Rome would wear.

Who else could it be, but God?

"So, where is she now?"

"She's on a journey with her companions right now, and having plenty of fun, by the sound of it."

"And Reiko?"

"She's already with her."

"Tch! So I'm late to the party… What about preparations with the god from over there?"

"That's already taken care of. Oh dear, I'm just going to be causing more trouble for her..."

"Good! Then send me over, if you please!"

"Understood. I hope you have a nice life there."

"Thanks for getting us taken care of then. See you!"

Though she'd been pretty spry for a ninety-year-old, her soul had grown weary over the years. But after she'd been freed from the restraints of her aging body, she was as energetic as she had been back in her younger days.

Her soul and consciousness were sent away to another world by the young man who looked like a god. After he was finished, he muttered to himself, "But still, I was so surprised when a normal human was able to contact me seventy years ago through sheer force of will... It really made me realize once again just how much potential they have. Definitely a learning experience, if I do say so myself."

The being who watched over Earth fondly remembered the promise the girls who came to yell at him had forced him to make...

We're going to have you make up for all the fun times I was supposed to have with Kaoru!

"I ended up causing more trouble for Celes again... I really must do something to make it up to her."

"Welcome to my world: Verny!"

Kyoko recoiled slightly as she came face-to-face with a girl, grinning from ear-to-ear.

"Um, so, about what the god from Earth and I talked about..."

"Yes, I've already heard all about it! Should be the same thing as what Reiko Kuon asked for, right?"

She looks excited about this... Kyoko thought to herself.

"So, uh...you seem pretty happy about something," she couldn't help but comment.

The goddess, on the other hand, seemed like she'd just been waiting to be asked that.

"Well, you see, I just got a message from the being in charge of your world, saying he's sorry to cause me trouble and that he's going to make it up to me somehow. Hehe... Ehehe..."

Kyoko knew exactly what was going on here. They didn't say you got wiser as you grew older for nothing.

"What did Reiko ask for?"

"She asked to 'be able to use every type of magic and to have unlimited MP.'"

Yeah, that sounds like Reiko all right. Just goes all in when it comes to this stuff.

"Then I'd like the ability to create anything I want."

"A-Anything? That might be a little *too* much..."

The goddess fretted. Thus, Kyoko conceded and changed her request.

"Then how about the ability for me to create any ship I know of? I'm no expert on ships, so I'd like to ask for them to be put together based on what's written about them. I'd also like to automatically know how to use each one I make, please. I'm a complete beginner when it comes to this stuff, after all."

"Only ships, you say... I think Kaoru and the others might be just about ready to cross the sea, actually, so this is some good timing. Let's go with that, then."

The goddess seemed relieved that she managed to have Kyoko scale back her wish to something more reasonable. Kyoko, on the other hand, was grinning on the inside.

"But you're quite the impressive pair. I've heard what you managed to do from the other god, despite the fact that you're only humans. Why did you go through such lengths to do that? Just who are you to Kaoru?"

Kyoko broke into a wide grin as she answered the goddess: "I'm Kyoko Nishizono, and she's Reiko Kuon—we're Kaoru Nagase's best friends!"

After descending unto the world in her new body, her youth restored, Kyoko checked her surroundings before creating a certain ship from her memories. It was controlled by an on-board computer with its own personality, had its own powerful laser weaponry, came with its own squadron of robot soldiers, and was jam-packed full of supplies in its storage bay. This was how she was going to travel the world to find Kaoru and the others.

Even if she didn't end up finding her friend, Reiko should be able to use some sort of wide-range sensor magic to try and find Kaoru. Once Reiko realized that Kyoko had arrived in this world as well, she should be able to find or contact Kyoko, so they could join up and look together. It wasn't like she was pressed for time, especially since she'd asked for the same conditions Kaoru had set for her new body, after hearing about it from the god of Earth.

Kyoko sat herself in the captain's chair and gave an order to the computer.

"Let's take off!"

Extra Story:
Kaoru's Splendid Life

Several months had passed since the peace talks had ended.

"Miss Kaoru, the Aligot Empire sent you an invitation to celebrate the construction of their first ship."

"Pass!" I immediately turned down the invitation when Francette told me about it.

The ship in question was based on a model I had given them: a carrack, a ship from the early Age of Sail, meant to traverse the open seas. It was a bit smaller than most of the carracks you'd find back on Earth, but it should be good enough for their first prototype. So long as it wasn't hit by a sudden storm or anything, it should be plenty to get them to the island to the west.

I understood why the brass in Aligot wanted to invite me out there, but if I was to be honest here, I just didn't want to go. I knew it was because they felt like they owed me a debt of gratitude for telling them about the island and empowering them with the knowledge about boats to get there. They probably invited me as a way of deepening our friendship and to ask me for more technical advice on shipbuilding, and I wasn't against that.

Still, so many had died in that battle. I bet there were just as many people who held a grudge against me as who were grateful for my efforts. They'd lost sons, husbands, and fathers in that war, and they weren't just going to forget all that and welcome me with open arms because I helped out their country just a little.

But it'd be a devastating blow for them if I was to suddenly disappear or turn my back on Aligot, so I doubted they'd try and harm me. That said, I also doubted that sort of deep-seated hatred would disappear so easily. That was why I thought it best for me to not go there, at least for now. They might never be able to bring themselves to forgive me, but their anger might at least fade over time. The passage of time could be cruel, but it could also end up being a blessing in disguise.

"Then for the next order of business, you've been invited to a party with a group of delegates from Aligot…"

"Oh, maybe I'll go to that one, actually. I'm sure those guys have their own standing to worry about, after all."

Even if it'd only been half a year, I still had experience working as an office lady. Also, as someone who was once a working adult, I knew a little something about what it meant to have "standing" in society. Their reputation back home could get much worse if they didn't meet with me before going back home, and I'd just feel bad for them if that happened. I'm actually a pretty considerate person, you see.

No, seriously, I mean it!

"You've also received an invitation to the crown prince of Aseed's birthday celebration…"

"Pass! I've got a bad feeling about that one. Wouldn't the king just say no to it, anyway?"

"Oh, well…yes, probably."

I'm sure the king would end up putting a stop to it himself, in the end, but I'd like to think that this was his way of consulting with me first before rejecting the invitation on my behalf… Or maybe he just didn't have the guts to do it, because he was afraid I'd find out he rejected it in my name.

"You've also received this message from the crown prince of Brancott—"

I swiped the letter from her hand and tore it to shreds on the spot.

"Wh-What are you doing?!" Francette exclaimed, panicking over the fact that I'd ripped up a letter from a royal without even reading it.

I don't care how many problems this causes, I'm gonna live the way I want to! There's no place for him in my new life here!

Francette's shoulders slumped as she watched me stomp on the scraps of paper I'd thrown on the ground. I had already talked all about the prince and his antics with Francette, so it should be fine.

"Next is something from a Mr. Elretz from the Republic of Leleyda…"

"Who? And wait, *where*?"

Gonna be honest here, I've never heard of those names before.

When Francette finally left, after passing on all the latest happenings from the palace, I finally had a chance to catch my breath. Ever since Lolotte had taken over my duties at the Maillart Workshop, I'd moved back into the house that the children lived in and made sure to take care of them. Well, I say "take care of," but Lucy was in charge of cooking after inheriting the position from Lolotte. If I did everything for them and ended up disappearing one day, it'd be hard for them to suddenly have to take care of themselves, otherwise.

I'd just help out every once in a while as their guardian, while the kids would do pretty much everything on their own. Other than that, they were completely independent.

They'd split up the cooking, cleaning, and laundry and did it all themselves, which was why I wasn't really doing anything at all. I just ended up lazing around the house when I came back home.

"Lunch is ready, Miss Kaoru!"

Yeah, not too shabby.

Wait...am I just a mooch now?

I only made enough money to support my own lifestyle, and they didn't even try to take a single copper coin from me... I wasn't just a mooch, but a NEET, too!

No! I was actually working! I was saving up money by selling my potions and producing new products alongside the Abili Trade Company, and I'd even had meetings with representatives from other countries... But that didn't matter, since I wasn't putting any of that money into our finances at home! I was just like those losers who put all their money into booze and gambling, without giving any to their families...

...Dang, now I'm depressed. Maybe I'll go out shopping, for a change...

I left the house and had just started walking to the shopping district when...

"Long time no see, Miss Kaoru!"

"Ah, Merliton..."

It was the engineer in charge of building ships for Aligot.

"Sorry to bother you, but there was something I wanted to ask you regarding the boats..."

Yeah, I should be able to help out with something like that. I'd told people not to come to me with their demands and requests before, but I was referring to my goddess powers. I didn't really mind helping people out with what I could do as the *human* Kaoru. There may not be much I could offer by way of help, but I'd gladly do what I could.

So long as it wasn't anything evil, anyway.

"So, who are those two?"

"Ah, pardon the late introductions:. This is Harsoth, an artist, and this is Garecles, a sculptor. We all came here together with the delegation sent to visit Balmore."

After exchanging greetings with my two new acquaintances, I headed over with them to the inn they were staying at, so we could talk things over. The delegates were being put up in guest rooms at the palace, of course, but the craftspeople that had come with them were staying at the inn. It made sense, since they weren't the guests of honor.

But I did wonder how the delegates felt when the craftsmen they had just so happened to bring along could meet with me this easily...

The craftsmen from the empire would stop by often to come and visit me. It seemed they took a liking to me after the peace talks, when I provided them with what they needed to build their boats (especially when I gave them the models for the ships and explained what they would need to fit them with), as well as giving them all that advice on farming and fishing and the like. They had to come to me since I wasn't going to Aligot myself, but I did kinda want to be around to see the ceremonial launch of their first prototype ship.

They might not even have that sort of tradition here, but I could *make* it a thing if I was there for it. They should totally get into it if I said it was some sort of ceremony to "give the ship the blessing of the Goddess" or something.

Merliton and the others had taken notes on questions from other Aligot professionals, and we all had a good time talking it over as they scribbled down my replies. It was a long trip back to Aligot, and it wasn't like it was completely free of danger, either. It was the least I could do for them, since they had come all this way to see me.

At the time, I didn't realize why Merliton had gone out of his way to bring an artist and a sculptor just to meet me. I didn't even notice the sparkling in their eyes as they looked at me...

It wasn't until much, *much* later that I heard rumors that the figureheads on the fronts of the Aligot Empire's fleet of ships all had the harshest looks in their eyes...

After saying my goodbyes to the people who'd come from the Aligot Empire, I was on my way back to town, when...

"Miss Kaoru!"

"Oh boy..."

The messenger from the crown prince of Brancott had made his appearance yet again. No matter how many times I told him to beat it, he just kept coming back...

"Please, we would be honored to have you visit our country! The prince is very much looking forward to seeing you!"

Well, I'm *not*...

If things ended up going south, I could end up stuck in Brancott for good. If they steered the conversation and began cross-examining me, I felt like I'd let slip who I really was pretty easily. So, you know. Discretion was the better part of valor, and all that.

"I don't have any plans on going to a country I know nothing about. I don't know what could happen to me there, and frankly, I don't *wanna* know. Well, I suppose it wouldn't be impossible if the king here ordered me to do it..."

"B-But then you'd claim the king didn't have the right to give you any orders…"

Exactly.

I'd sworn to the Goddess that I'd never listen to what the important bigwigs or the royal family had to say. Which was why I'd just flat-out refuse any sort of order from the king, if he ever tried to give me one. So even if the king demanded that I go, then I'd use that as the very reason *not* to. It was a pretty funny catch-22 that actually worked in my favor.

Maybe I'd ask the king to try and order me to do something when I got the chance. I said I might think about it, if the king gave the order, but I didn't say anything about actually going. I'd just tell them that I wouldn't attend *after* thinking it over, that was all. See? That way, I wouldn't be lying.

Wait, that's it! If the king orders me to go meet with the prince of Brancott, then I wouldn't have to see him ever again, since it'd break the oath I made to the Goddess… Maybe I will actually try asking him to do that, next time I see him.

After I chased the messenger away and headed into town…

"Miss Kaoru!"

Really?

"We would be honored to have you come visit Brancott…"

Seemed this guy was here for something different than the last one.

Apparently, he was a messenger from the crown prince's brother, Ghislain. He'd heard I was avoiding his big brother, and that maybe this could be his chance to shack up with the angel of the goddess and take Fernand's place as next in line for the throne.

...Ugh, my head hurts.

This guy had to have heard about me at the palace, right? Then he should already know I had no interest whatsoever in royalty. And besides, the prince was basically conspiring to usurp the throne, which was something that'd only come back to bite him in the end, and hard. I didn't want any part of that, thank you very much.

"I have no plans to help him usurp the throne. If you try talking to me again about this, I'm gonna take it up with the crown prince himself and tell him that I'm too scared to come to Brancott because the second prince's messenger is harassing me."

I wasn't going to complain to the little brother—but Fernand himself.

The messenger could only stand there, their mouth opening and closing, with no words coming out.

Well, yeah. He'd be as good as dead if I really did that, after all.

After driving away both of the messengers, I was finally on my way to the shopping district when...

"Miss Kaoru!"

Gah!

"Are you heading out? Then I'll come with you, too!"

"Oh, it's you, Lilil..."

She was the daughter of Johann, the guy who ran the Abili Trade Company, and the girl whose illness I cured using a potion a while back. For some reason, I ended up bumping into her pretty often whenever I went out.

...Like, *really* often. She's not keeping tabs on what I'm doing and *waiting* for me, right...? Nah, that can't be right.

I was probably just overthinking things… Probably.

"Ah, Kaoru!"

Agh, the local kids! They were my worthy rivals whenever we played marbles together. So much so that I'd actually lost more than I'd won against them.

"Are you going out, Kaol?"

Oho, she brought her little sister today! Man, little Latori is such a cutie…

"You going shopping, Kaoru?"

"Where are you going, Carol?"

"Oh, Miss Kaoru!"

"Kaoru!"

"Lady Kaoru!"

AAARRRGGGHHH!!!

I can't get through to the shopping district with all you people in the way! Just gimme a break already…

But, you know… It might not be so bad to keep this lifestyle up for a little while longer…

Afterword

Hi, everyone, it's FUNA. Thanks for picking up the next volume in the series!

...No one just skipped the first volume before buying this one, right?

We covered everything from the war against Aligot, the most action-intense part of season one of "I Shall Survive Using Potions!" to the start of Kaoru's new journey. What's going to end up happening to Kaoru and company?

The first volume of this series managed to stay in the top twenty for Oricon's book rankings after it came out, and it even received a second printing run.

This is all because of you guys! Thank you so much! It's all thanks to you we got the second volume of this series out. Here's hoping we can keep this up for volume three and onward...

Actually, two days before writing this, I tripped and smacked my head against the corner of a bookshelf. The area around my left eye got all swollen, and it looked just like those huge black eyes characters get in manga and stuff. Man, did I laugh and laugh... You know, after I was busy being scared half to death.

Eyes and hands are the most important parts for book lovers like me...

I'm writing using only one eye right now. Sometimes I'm a one-eyed author, and other times I'm someone else entirely…

Volume one of the manga by Kokonoe Hibiki-san should be coming out around the same time as this book! Get yourself to a place that sells them! Go, go, go!

There's so many people I want to thank, so I'll do it all at once.

Thank you to my editors, Sukima-sama, my illustrator, the people in charge of proofreading and revising my stuff, and even everyone involved with printing, publishing, and distributing the book, the bookstores that decided to carry it, the people on the novel site I posted the original story on who would give me comments, advice, and point out errors—and, most of all, thank YOU from the bottom of my heart for picking up this book! Thank you all so much!

I'm looking forward to your support for the manga as well, and I hope to see you all in the next volume!

…There *is* going to be a next volume, right?

Our real fight starts now!!!

I SHALL
SURVIVE USING
P🧪TIONS!

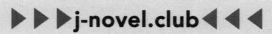

J-Novel Club Lineup

Ebook Releases Series List

Altina the Sword Princess
An Archdemon's Dilemma:
    How to Love Your Elf Bride
Arifureta Zero
Arifureta: From Commonplace
    to World's Strongest
Ascendance of a Bookworm
Beatless
Bibliophile Princess
By the Grace of the Gods
Campfire Cooking in Another World
    with My Absurd Skill
Can Someone Please Explain What's
    Going On?!
The Combat Baker and Automaton Waitress
Cooking with Wild Game
Crest of the Stars
Demon King Daimaou
Demon Lord, Retry!
Der Werwolf: The Annals of Veight
The Economics of Prophecy
The Faraway Paladin
Full Metal Panic!
The Greatest Magicmaster's Retirement Plan
Grimgar of Fantasy and Ash
Her Majesty's Swarm
The Holy Knight's Dark Road
How a Realist Hero Rebuilt the Kingdom
How NOT to Summon a Demon Lord
I Refuse to Be Your Enemy!
I Saved Too Many Girls and Caused the
    Apocalypse
I Shall Survive Using Potions!
If It's for My Daughter, I'd Even Defeat a
    Demon Lord
In Another World With My Smartphone
Infinite Dendrogram
Infinite Stratos
Invaders of the Rokujouma!?
Isekai Rebuilding Project
JK Haru is a Sex Worker in Another World
Kobold King
Kokoro Connect
Last and First Idol
Lazy Dungeon Master
The Magic in this Other World is
    Too Far Behind!
The Master of Ragnarok & Blesser of Einherjar
Middle-Aged Businessman, Arise in Another
    World!
Mixed Bathing in Another Dimension

My Next Life as a Villainess: All Routes Lead
    to Doom!
Otherside Picnic
Outbreak Company
Outer Ragna
Record of Wortenia War
Seirei Gensouki: Spirit Chronicles
Seriously Seeking Sister! Ultimate Vampire
    Princess Just Wants Little Sister; Plenty of
    Service Will Be Provided!
Sexiled: My Sexist Party Leader Kicked
    Me Out, So I Teamed Up With a Mythical
    Sorceress!
Sorcerous Stabber Orphen:
    The Wayward Journey
The Tales of Marielle Clarac
Tearmoon Empire
Teogonia
There Was No Secret Evil-Fighting
    Organization (srsly?!), So I Made One
    MYSELF!
The Underdog of the Eight Greater Tribes
The Unwanted Undead Adventurer
Welcome to Japan, Ms. Elf!
The White Cat's Revenge as Plotted from the
    Dragon King's Lap
The World's Least Interesting Master
    Swordsman

Manga Series:

A Very Fairy Apartment
An Archdemon's Dilemma:
    How to Love Your Elf Bride
Animeta!
Ascendance of a Bookworm
Cooking with Wild Game
Demon Lord, Retry!
Discommunication
The Faraway Paladin
How a Realist Hero Rebuilt the Kingdom
I Shall Survive Using Potions!
Infinite Dendrogram
The Magic in this Other World is
    Too Far Behind!
Marginal Operation
The Master of Ragnarok & Blesser of Einherjar
Seirei Gensouki: Spirit Chronicles
Sorcerous Stabber Orphen:
    The Reckless Journey
Sweet Reincarnation
The Unwanted Undead Adventurer